Coin Laundries
—
Road to Financial Independence

A Complete Guide to Starting and Operating Profitable Self-Service Laundries

Emerson G. Higdon

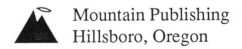
Mountain Publishing
Hillsboro, Oregon

Published by Mountain Publishing
P. O. Box 1747
Hillsboro, Oregon 97123

Printed in the United States of America
93 92 91 90 89 8 7 6 5 4 3 2 1

Library of Congress Cataloging-in-Publication Data

Higdon, Emerson G., 1933-
    Coin laundries—road to financial independence : a complete guide
to starting and operating profitable self-service laundries /
Emerson G. Higdon.
        p.   cm.
    Includes index.
    ISBN 0-9623173-8-1 : $29.95
    1. Self-service laundries—Management. 2. New business
enterprises—Management. I. Title.
HD9999.L382H54 1989
649'.1'068—dc20   89-12815
                                                                CIP

NOTICE

THIS BOOK is not a "get rich quick" scheme. Although money can be made in the self-service, coin-operated laundry business, it requires a combination of skill, adequate financing, and years of hard work. Even then there may be unforseen circumstances that can cause a business to fail.

This book does not guaranteed success. There are great financial risks in starting or buying a business. Anyone who invests time and money in a business must do so realizing that they risk losing their investment.

This book does not cover every situation that the reader may encounter when starting, buying, or running a business. Its purpose is to inform and entertain—not to give professional advice. Contact an attorney, an accountant, or other professional help before investing <u>any</u> time or money in a business venture.

Neither the author nor the publisher guarantee the accuracy of the information contained in this book. Although every effort was made to maintain a high standard of accuracy at the time of publication, there may be errors. Some of the information may now be outdated.

ABOUT THE AUTHOR

EMERSON G. "SKIP" HIGDON was a Branch Manager for an international appliance manufacturer before resigning to become an entrepreneur. After leaving corporate life, he started and operated several successful small businesses.

One of these businesses was a modern self-service laundry near Portland, Oregon. Nine months after its grand opening, Higdon's laundry was the highest volume coin laundry in the state!

Higdon has also designed coin laundries, sold coin laundry equipment, and acted as a consultant to other industry entrepreneurs. In this book he shares with you all the secrets of owning and operating successful coin laundries.

At 55, Higdon is semi-retired, devoting his time to writing, consulting, and adventuring with this wife Joan of thirty-three years.

CONTENTS

Contents

1

HOW MUCH MONEY CAN I MAKE?

YOU CAN BECOME a millionaire! Many owners and operators of self-service coin laundries have done it. Some have become rich with one giant store situated in an outstanding location. Others have made their fortune by operating several smaller self-service laundries in good locations.

The opportunity to make big money with self-service laundries is better today than ever before. Self-service laundries have changed considerably since their beginnings in the 1930's. Then, laundry owners used wringer washers with coin slides. Now this industry has turned into a $3 billion a year business in quarters, dimes, and nickels, and it's still growing.

There are over 1,000 new self-service laundries opening each year in the United States. This is a rate of 2.7 new laundries per day. In addition to this, smart investors are buying up older, run-down laundries all over the country, and converting them into modern, highly-profitable businesses.

Coin Laundries — Road to Financial Independence

From the late 1950's until the mid-1970's, there was a decline in the construction of <u>new</u> self-service laundries. Owner neglect turned the existing ones into rundown, dirty, and undesirable places to wash clothes. As a result, self-service laundries developed a bad image. Although many of them were profitable, the glamour was gone. Investment dollars went elsewhere.

In the past few years, the picture has changed. Investment dollars are pouring back into this industry in greater amounts than ever before. A new breed of dynamic business person is opening, managing, and profiting from coin laundry stores. Equipment manufacturers are developing new "state of the art" equipment to meet the needs of the modern coin laundry. Shopping center owners are courting laundry owners, and equipment distributors are gearing up to serve this growing industry.

What has changed? The market. There is now a vast and increasing number of single people living alone. There is also a huge increase in single-parent families who cannot justify or afford the large cash outlay for a laundry pair. A significant percentage of our population is becoming a society of highly-mobile apartment dwellers, and a large number of these apartments have inadequate laundry facilities, if any.

The number of working mothers is also increasing dramatically. Many would rather spend two hours in a coin laundry than eight hours doing laundry at home. The prices of laundry appliances have risen sharply in the past few years as has the cost of appliance repair, making it difficult for people to afford their own appliances.

Finally, financial priorities have shifted. Forget about necessities. People want personal gratification <u>now</u>! If it's a choice between a boat and a laundry pair, the boat often wins.

What about the future? Are there long term opportunities to make money? Yes! According to economists and sociologists, these trends will continue. The need for good self-service laundries should continue too.

Success rarely comes easily. Most self-service laundry owners who succeed in making big money do so through trial and error, sometimes called "the school of hard knocks." Those who survive their mistakes go on to achieve great financial security, independence, and recognition as outstanding business people. Others go broke.

Why don't they all become rich? It all boils down to one thing—lack of knowledge. But where can you turn for knowledge? Manufacturers? They must sell their products or they are out of business. Distributors? They, too, must sell their products and services or they fail. You might talk to other laundry owners—your future competitors. But would they <u>really</u> help you?

What about your attorney, or your accountant? An attorney understands the law, and an accountant can read and interpret figures. But this does not necessarily make them good business consultants in an unfamiliar industry. Until now, there really hasn't been anyone to turn to for good information where a conflict of interest or lack of knowledge didn't exist.

For years, I watched countless self-service laundries fail, operate at a loss, or produce minimal profit because the owners were misled by bad advice. This book (the only one of its type in existence) covers the self-service coin laundry business, in detail, from A to Z. It fills the gap between you and potential profits by giving you all the information you need to reap the financial rewards of a successful coin laundry business.

If you plan to purchase a self-service laundry, this book will tell you how. If you plan to build a self-service laundry, this book will guide you every step of the way. You will learn:

- How to find a good business location and evaluate its potential.
- All about the advantages and disadvantages of buying an existing business compared to starting a new one.
- How to evaluate an existing business.
- How to avoid costly pitfalls when starting or buying a business.
- How to negotiate with a business owner from a position of power.

- How to verify the profit of an existing business without relying on the owner's books.
- How to estimate the profits from a new business.
- How to conduct a market survey and effectively use the information to make money.
- How to plan and build a modern, highly-profitable coin-operated laundry.
- How to evaluate, select, and save money on the purchase of coin-operated laundry equipment.
- How to negotiate a lease to your advantage and prevent future problems with the landlord.
- How to estimate equipment, construction, and operating costs.
- Tips on saving tens of thousands of dollars on these costs.
- How to find and work with qualified contractors and sub-contractors.
- How to develop an operating plan that shows you exactly how profitable an existing business is, or a new business will be.
- How to develop and evaluate your financial statements for greater profit.
- How to get affordable financing that will meet your needs.
- How to save thousands of dollars in advertising while substantially increasing your business volume.

In addition to this, you will find valuable information on security, maintenance, repair, accounting procedures, energy conservation, and laundry management, as well as tips on how and when to hire professional assistance. Save $30,000 to $50,000 (or more) by applying the information contained in this book!

If you are looking for a business to buy or build, this book will help you. If you are already a successful self-service laundry owner, this book will help you become even more successful. While success is not guaranteed, this book does provide a detailed, step-by-step plan to help you attain it. It will eliminate many costly mistakes that could well mean the difference between success and total failure. In business, what you don't know can (and most likely will) hurt you.

Many speak the truth when they say that they despise riches, but they mean the riches possessed by other men.

—Charles Caleb Colton (1780–1832)

Coin Laundries — Road to Financial Independence

I've been rich and I've been poor; rich is better.

—Sophie Tucker

2

IS THE COIN-OPERATED LAUNDRY BUSINESS FOR ME?

LET'S LOOK AT the advantages of owning and operating a self-service laundry:

- Good market stability
- Limited competition
- Good cash flow
- Unlimited opportunity
- Good pre-tax net profit
- Simplicity

GOOD MARKET STABILITY

Like housing and food, clean clothes are a necessity. Everyone must have clean clothes. The demand for clean clothes is as strong when the economy is bad as it is when the economy is good. People may go without an automobile, new clothes, luxury or leisure items, but they are not going to run around in dirty clothes.

Coin Laundries — Road to Financial Independence

LIMITED COMPETITION

There has been a big shift toward mass merchandising in the last 20 years, driving many small retailers out of business. With their tremendous clout, big chains can sell products at prices lower than the cost of these same products to independent merchants. This makes it difficult for small, independent entrepreneurs to succeed.

Hardware stores, drugstores, appliance stores, clothing stores, restaurants, grocery stores, pet stores, and others have been affected by the sphere of influence of the big chains. But this is not so with the self-service coin laundry as you will see. No one in the industry can make a better purchase than you when it comes to machinery, natural gas, electricity, water, rent, construction, and the hiring of people.

GOOD CASH FLOW

Money is not tied up in inventory in the self-service laundry business because little (if any) inventory is required. It's a cash business, so there are no bad check problems, the plague of the retail industry. There are no accounts receivable, so no uncollectible accounts or late payment problems. You will never have to repossess a load of washed clothes. If cash runs short, wait several hours and open the coin boxes. The quarters accumulate like snowflakes on cold concrete!

UNLIMITED OPPORTUNITY

Anyone—from college student to retiree—can be highly successful owning and operating a self-service coin laundry. You can devote all or part of your time to your business. With proper management, you can still have a fair amount of freedom to pursue other interests. You can stay small and highly profitable, or you can build a multi-store, multi-million dollar corporation. No matter which you choose, *your opportunities are unlimited.*

Is the Coin-Operated Laundry Business for Me?

GOOD PRE-TAX NET PROFIT

Net profit at a well-run coin laundry can range from 25 to 35 percent pre-tax. Some have gone higher than 40 percent. Compare this with other service or retail businesses!

Take a look at this monthly profit statement of a medium-size coin laundry:

AVERAGE MONTHLY PROFIT STATEMENT

Gross Sales
Washers and Dryers (32 @ 6 Cycles Per Day)	$5,800	
Other Vending	660	
Total Gross Sales		$6,460

Operating Expenses
Rent	$1,385	
Utilities	1,160	
Product for Vending	200	
Insurance	200	
Advertising	150	
Maintenance and Repair	75	
Operating Supplies	40	
Depreciation (Actual)	600	
Interest on Loan (Flat Rate)	335	
Miscellaneous	100	
Total Expenses		4,245

Net Profit Before Taxes	$2,215

If this coin laundry required $30,000 as a down payment, it would earn $2,215 per month. Compare this to the earnings that would be generated by $30,000 at present bank interest rates!

SIMPLICITY

Because there is very little (if any) inventory, self-service laundries have no inventory taxes, inventory theft, obsolete inventory, inventory close-outs, inventory handling and storage costs, damaged inventory write-offs, inventory insurance, or complicated inventory accounting procedures.

There are no accounts receivable, so there are no collection problems or records to keep. There are few accounts payable, and these require only a minimum of records and attention. You can devote your time to things that increase your net profit.

Self-service laundries can be run without employees. This means no payroll, payroll taxes, payroll accounting, or employee theft. When properly managed, unattended self-service laundries are simple, highly-profitable businesses.

Is this business for you? Before answering, read on.

3

THE MODERN
SELF-SERVICE
LAUNDRY

COIN LAUNDRIES HAVE changed considerably over the years. The interior decorating in some puts many expensive homes to shame. Matching woodwork, wallpaper, lush carpet, decorator ceilings, and fine furniture can be found in many. Some stores boast decorator lighting, hanging plants, and framed pictures. Ample background lighting makes these coin laundries visible and attractive to people as far away as the street.

Some laundries have a comfortable lounge area for their customers. Vending machines dispense popcorn, soft drinks, coffee, candy-bars, sandwiches and a variety of snack foods. VCR's and large screen television sets are featured at other self-service laundries. Many even have an enclosed area with juvenile furniture and toys for children to keep them from annoying customers.

Modern coin laundries vary in size from a few washers and dryers to several hundred machines. One laundry located near the

Coin Laundries — Road to Financial Independence

city center in Denver, Colorado has over 450 washers and dryers and covers an entire block! On weekends, it's not unusual to see over 300 people in the laundry at the same time. This self-service laundry has been continuously under expansion since 1980, and a snack bar is now being added.

A self-service laundry in Ames, Iowa has a snack bar and pub where university students can eat and sip "suds" while washing their clothes. This laundry is so successful that the owner, a student at the university, started a national franchise that has made him millions!

Several self-service laundries in Texas feature a band for Friday night entertainment. They have developed into social centers where people can meet while doing their laundry.

Self-service laundries offer many opportunities for creative layout and interior design. Manufacturers and distributors of coin laundry equipment can provide you with pictures and drawings of various arrangements. The next time you pass an old, rundown laundry, stop and look in. Apply a little mental creativity to the interior layout and decor. You could be looking at a potential gold mine!

Equipment can be arranged in a variety of ways to provide an attractive and functional layout. Instead of a row of washers on one wall and a row of dryers down the other, many laundries have the washers and dryers arranged in convenient groups. Each group consists of two washers and a stacked dryer (two regular size dryers stacked on top of each other) placed back-to-back with two more washers and another stacked dryer. A clothes-folding table is located next to the dryers. Comfortable seating and plenty of lighting is provided near each group. This allows customers to wash, dry, and fold their clothes in well-lighted, comfortable surroundings without being overrun by other people.

Attendants at some coin laundries wash, dry, fold, and package a customer's laundry for a small fee. Many laundries offer a one-stop clothes care service of economy bulk dry-cleaning or professional dry-cleaning along with the self-service laundry.

The Modern Self-Service Laundry

Some higher-volume stores have a drive-up window so customers can deliver and pick up their clothes without having to park. This is especially convenient in areas subject to bad weather.

Many laundry owners have been successful in combining their laundries with other businesses, such as convenience stores, taverns, or fast food restaurants. The result is increased customer traffic for both.

Today's modern coin laundry generates mountains of quarters for the owner. A police officer on patrol late one night spotted a man acting suspiciously in a shopping center parking lot. He was trying to load a large canvas bag into the trunk of a big Buick. He pulled and tugged at the bag, trying to get it from the ground to the bumper. He finally rolled it over the lip, and into the trunk. The rear of the Buick dropped seven inches.

The officer approached the man to investigate and found that the bag contained about 20,000 quarters. The "suspect," who owned the laundry in the shopping center, had just finished emptying his machines and was taking his haul home to count. Stunned, the officer suggested that this was dangerous, particularly at night. He asked the man if he wasn't concerned about someone running off with his money. "Officer, anyone who can run off with this bag can have it!"

Successful businesses don't occur by accident. They take a lot of careful planning and hard work. For the beginning entrepreneur, starting a new business is like trying to negotiate a mine field without a map. One wrong move can spell disaster. Read the following chapters carefully. They provide the map that will take you safely through the mine field to success!

Coin Laundries — Road to Financial Independence

> Yesterday is a cancelled check; tomorrow is a promissory note; today is the only cash you have—so spend it wisely.
>
> —Kay Lyons

4

SELECTING
YOUR LOCATION

LOCATION IS CRITICAL to the success or failure of a retail business. Consider what might happen if you selected a poor location for a large self-service laundry. You sign a lease for a ten-year commitment of over a quarter million dollars with a monthly lease payment of $2,083. You prepare the space for the equipment at a cost of $35,000. This includes plumbing, electrical, sheet metal, and carpentry. Next, you purchase equipment and install it at a cost of $100,000. You open your laundry and your business grows rapidly for the first six months. After that it levels off, and no amount of advertising increases the revenue. Your monthly gross revenue falls $300 short of paying your lease and utility expenses.

If you close your business, you must still pay $2,083 each month to the landlord. You might sublease the space or declare bankruptcy. You could run the business at a loss, put $300 a month into it from savings, and hope for a miracle. Even if the space is sublet, you cannot recover the $35,000 in materials and labor for the plumbing, electrical, sheet metal, and carpentry work. What about your equipment? You could use your equipment at another (better) location or sell it at a fraction of the original cost.

If this scares you, it should. Selecting a bad location can be extremely costly. A manufacturer, a distributor, a consultant, a leasing agent, or the owner of a shopping center may tell you that a particular location is good; but if it's not, <u>you</u> and you alone will pay the price. In this chapter you will learn how to pick a location that will ensure your success.

THE GENERAL LOCATION

When you look for a business location, you must ask and answer the following questions:

- <u>Who</u> are your prospective customers?
- <u>What</u> are their needs?
- <u>When</u> will they be in need of your product or service?
- <u>Where</u> are they presently getting the product or service?
- <u>Why</u> should they buy from you?

If you plan to build or purchase a self-service laundry in a <u>metropolitan area</u>, consider the following when comparing locations:

- Population Demographics
- Competition
- Market Trends

Population Demographics

The ideal location for a high-volume self-service laundry is a <u>very</u> densely populated area consisting of working people whose earnings are classified as medium-to low-income. There should be a high percentage of both single-family and multiple-family rental dwellings. Make sure the area has a heavy concentration of younger people in their childbearing years. An older population of retired people creates very little business for a self-service laundry.

Look for a heavy concentration of families as opposed to single people. A significant portion of the population must be children, and the projected birth rate should be higher than average. Remember, in this business dirt is your ally, and children create "mountains" of dirty clothes. A high birth rate guarantees future business by providing a continuous supply of dirt-attracting children.

Neighborhoods with lots of apartments and rental houses usually attract a highly-mobile group of people who often cannot afford their own laundry appliances. Many rely on a friend, their parents, or a self-service laundry. This is particularly true for single-family dwellers where central laundry facilities of an apartment complex are not available.

Competition

If you see a number of self-service laundries in the vicinity, you can be reasonably sure that you are on the right track. This means there are a lot of self-service laundry users in the area. If these laundries are old and rundown, so much the better. If they are modern, well-run laundries and you are inexperienced, you may be wise to look elsewhere.

If you find a good location with a number of old, rundown laundries in the area, go for it! Buy one and remodel. If the owners won't sell, build a new one. A modern self-service laundry will capture most of the customers, causing the rundown laundries to become unprofitable and close. The remaining customers will be yours. Remember this: A well-managed self-service coin laundry with an ongoing modernization program is the best deterrent to competition.

What if the apartments in the area provide central laundry facilities for their tenants? The tenants may still be prospects for a good self-service laundry. Visit every apartment complex in the area and look for these problems. If you find them, you can count on dissatisfied tenants:

- Laundry room dirty and/or poorly lit
- Outdated or broken equipment
- Insufficient washers and dryers to meet demand
- Theft of clothes from laundry room
- Removal of clothes from machines by other tenants
- Fear of harm due to poor laundry room security
- Laundry room hours incompatible with tenants' schedules

Market Trends

Thoroughly research market trends before you make a final decision on location. It's easy to see the location today, but you must also visualize what it will be like during the eighth, ninth, and tenth years of your lease. Carefully consider the answers to the following questions:

- Are dwellings being replaced by businesses?
- Are single family rental units being replaced by large, modern apartments with modern laundry facilities?
- Is the average age of the population increasing, decreasing, or stable?
- Is the quality of life in the area improving, deteriorating, or remaining stable?
- Will the area become more or less attractive to the small real estate investor who owns a few single-family rental-houses?
- Are the neighborhoods generally well-maintained, or are there signs of creeping urban blight?

Not all good laundry locations are in urban areas. Some highly-successful coin laundries are located in small towns or the sub-urbs. A coin laundry in a densely-populated area might draw most of its customers from just a few blocks away, but a laundry in a small town could draw from a 20-to 30-mile radius if the town has good shopping facilities.

If your location happens to be a resort area, look for a large seasonal tourist business. Coin laundries in towns where businesses serve a large agricultural industry might get a lot of business from migrant workers during certain times of the year. Business volume may be lower for laundries in less-populated areas, but so is the rent. And rent is a major expense.

Colleges and universities can provide a huge clientele for a modern self-service laundry if the following conditions exist:

1. Most of the students live in dormitories or in off-campus housing.
2. Laundry facilities are not provided by the school.
3. If they are, they don't meet students' needs.
4. Existing coin laundries in the area don't meet students' needs.

Make sure you do a thorough market survey in and around the campus. If the laundry doesn't draw students, it will have few customers.

After you select a general location, your next step is to select your store site.

THE STORE SITE

The High-Volume Supermarket

Look for store sites next to high-volume supermarkets. Supermarkets share the same customers as laundries because laundry customers all buy food on a regular basis. The greater the volume at the supermarket, the greater the potential for laundry customers.

Parking

Many coin laundries fail because they lack convenient parking. Customers simply will not carry big bundles of clothes for great distances, particularly in bad weather. They'd sooner find another laundry. Make sure there are enough parking spaces for all your customers when your laundry is operating at capacity. Don't base your need for parking spaces on an average requirement. If customers can't find parking on high-volume days, you could lose over 50 percent of your potential revenue.

Warning: Be careful about locating next to restaurants, beauty salons, or other businesses where people park and spend a lot of time. On high-volume days when your customers can't find parking, they will find other laundries.

Sometimes you can get your landlord to designate a fixed number of parking spaces for your laundry by painting the space or by signs. Negotiate this with the landlord before you sign the lease. Even so, designated spaces still require a considerable amount of policing on a day-to-day basis. If ample parking is not consistently available, find another store site.

Visual Exposure

Pick a store site that has good visual exposure. Make sure that potential customers can see your self-service laundry from the parking lot or the street. Good visual exposure means that fewer advertising dollars will be required to build your business and maintain the volume.

Look for a high percentage of window area. This allows customers to see the complete interior of the laundry as they approach. This not only attracts customers, but it gives them a sense of security to be able to see who is inside before they enter.

Shopping Patterns

As creatures of habit, people develop shopping patterns. Your customers tend to shop for goods and services in a direction toward their places of employment or toward the major urban center. Because of this, it's not unusual for a coin laundry to draw customers from five to six miles in one direction and from only a few blocks in another. Watch for these patterns when you are looking for your store site.

Selecting Your Location

Try to locate your laundry <u>between</u> your customers and their places of employment or where they shop. Picture your market as a long skinny oval with your laundry located near one end. This is the end closest to the major urban area or to the major area of employment. The oval stretches along the main traffic thoroughfare that carries people to work or to the places they shop. If your store site is at a major intersection, so much the better. It will then have two such ovals as its market.

Zoning Laws

Be sure the site you are considering is zoned for a self-service laundry. If not, you must petition for a zone change or look elsewhere. Getting a zone reclassified is like wading through glue. It takes great patience. If the store site is in a shopping center, ask the owner or leasing agent for help. They often have good contacts with local government officials and can get the job done faster.

Utilities

Your store site will require sewer, water, gas and/or electrical services. These services must meet your requirements, the equipment manufacturer's specifications, and local building codes. Make sure that the building codes and the manufacturer's specifications do not conflict. If they do, install your equipment according to the local building code.

If the equipment will not operate properly when installed according to code, the problem must be worked out between the equipment manufacturer and the government agency involved. This situation is rare, but it has happened. You may want to consider using a different brand of equipment.

If all this sounds complicated, it's not. Government agencies are usually very helpful when properly approached. Their advice is not only valuable, it's free. Use the following as a guide when looking at store sites:

Sewer Line

A four-inch sewer line will generally handle up to 30 standard-size washers, and a six-inch sewer line will handle up to 100. These figures may vary depending on the plumbing codes in the area. In rural areas, a septic tank system may be necessary if municipal sewer service is not available.

Before signing a lease, have the local plumbing inspector tell you the number of washers he will allow in your store. A four-inch line will normally handle over 30 washers, but what if all the stores in the center are using the same sewer line? The inspector may reduce this number drastically.

What if the sewer won't handle your requirements? You may have to run a new sewer line from your laundry to the main line in the street. Don't wait until after the lease is signed to learn that it will cost an extra $15,000 to tear up the parking lot.

Water Tap

At 60 pounds per square inch pressure, a 1½-inch diameter water line should serve up to 30 standard-size washers. A 2-inch line should serve up to 60 standard-size washers. Local building codes, however, will be the final determining factor.

Electrical Service

This should be 240-volt in either single-phase or three-phase current. Normally this is what is supplied. If only 120-volt service is available, be careful when selecting your equipment. Some manufacturers do not make equipment that will operate on 120 volts.

Sometimes 208-volt service is supplied. Refer to the equipment specification sheets and be sure to buy equipment that will operate on 208 volts. Both 240-volt and 208-volt service can be split to run equipment requiring 120-volt service.

Most self-service laundry equipment requires only single-phase current. If a dry-cleaning machine is to be included, three-phase current may be necessary for some makes or models.

Selecting Your Location

Natural Gas

Natural gas should be available to the store site. If not, contact the gas company. If natural gas is not available, you must depend on liquid propane gas or electricity for hot water and to heat the dryer drums. Your selection will depend on which energy source is the least expensive.

Natural gas requirements generally range from two-to four-million B.t.u. The gas company will size the meter and incoming line to supply the volume of gas that is needed to run your dryers and your hot water heater during peak load times.

Space Configuration

Store sites, like people, come in all different sizes and shapes. Each offers many layout and design possibilities. Coin laundries have been built in just about every size and shape imaginable. An area the shape of a square or rectangle is most common.

Occasionally a landlord or leasing agent will try to push an odd size, hard-to-lease location onto an inexperienced prospect. A coin laundry could be built in a space 10 feet wide by 120 feet long, but the customers would probably feel that they were doing their laundry in an alley. There are situations in which this space might be acceptable, but it's best to stay clear of dimensional extremes.

Forecasting Trends

A store site may meet all the requirements for a good site today, but what about the future? For example, road improvements can close roads for months—sometimes years. Local improvements in services (such as roads or parks) can result in large tax levies. New expressways or bridges can divert traffic from your area. Don't look to your government for financial damages— you won't get any.

Zoning can be changed. Your customers' dwellings can be replaced by factories, warehouses, or retail businesses. Smaller municipalities can be annexed by larger ones—resulting in increased taxes. A large employer can close or move out of the area.

Utility costs in one municipality can increase substantially while the same costs remain unchanged for a competitor in another area.

Careful forecasting is necessary before you sign a long-term lease. Avoid surprises and so-called "bad luck." Do your homework. Spend some time with your local government agencies. Get to know them. Haunt the local Planning Commission in particular. Don't forget to spend time with the utility companies. They are usually aware of development plans in your area.

THE SHOPPING CENTER VERSUS A FREE-STANDING STORE

Stores can either be free-standing or in a shopping center. Although rent is generally higher, a shopping center location has several advantages over a free-standing store:

- It draws more customers and from greater distances.
- It offers greater exposure to potential customers.
- Customers can shop while doing their laundry.
- Customers feel more secure, particularly at night.
- Advertising has greater impact for stores in a center.

If there is no shopping center in the area, a free-standing self-service laundry is your only alternative. You may want to reconsider the location if the area is densely-populated and there is no shopping center serving the people. Before you proceed with a free-standing laundry, think about this:

- Why haven't shopping center developers invested their money in that location?
- Where are the people presently doing their shopping, particularly for food?
- Where are they presently doing their laundry?

Selecting Your Location

If a thorough investigation proves that a good market exists for a self-service laundry, then by all means proceed with a free-standing store.

EVALUATING A SHOPPING CENTER

Evaluate a shopping center as a prospective store site carefully. There are good shopping centers and there are inferior ones. There is no end to the problems that a poorly managed center can create for a laundry owner. Be careful. For better or for worse, you are stuck with the lease.

Like people, shopping centers can get sick and die. It's difficult to maintain a good business in a shopping center that is run-down, with trash blowing in the parking lot and a lot of vacant space. A coin laundry in such a center is vulnerable. A competitor who opens a laundry in a good center will take your customers. People go where the action is.

Consider this when evaluating a shopping center:

- Is the shopping center clean, attractive, and well-managed?
- Does the center serve the peoples' needs, or must they go elsewhere?
- Have you obtained market demographics from the leasing agent?
- Are the entries and exits convenient? In all directions of travel?
- What is the traffic count on the streets bordering the center?
- Is there a sign listing all the stores? Is it highly visible?
- What are the marketing plans? Long-term? Short-term?
- What is the vacancy rate? Is it increasing or declining?
- What is the sales volume of the anchor grocery store?
- How much time is left on the grocery store lease?
- Are the stores in the center well-managed?
- Does the center have ample parking?
- Does the center serve patrons of nearby motels?

- Is there a strong merchants' association?
- Is the center making money for the owner?

You have many sources available to you for information that will help you locate your business. Among these are the local chamber of commerce, shopping center owners (managers), commercial real estate leasing agents, and the utilities that serve the area. Be sure to contact the government agencies involved in municipal planning, road maintenance, road construction, water service, sewer service, zoning, building construction, and building inspection.

Your local post office can supply carrier route maps. These will provide statistics showing distribution of population and population density. Newspapers often publish market reviews with valuable statistics. Use the library. It's an excellent source of information on just about everything.

What are the three biggest influences on the success of your laundry? Location! location! location! Take your time and find the right location. Your financial future is at stake. Don't trust others to find your location for you. If you do, chances are you'll be sorry.

5

BUYING
VERSUS BUILDING

IF YOU PURCHASE an existing laundry, you save much of the cost of plumbing, electrical, and sheet metal work. These costs can range from $20,000 to $30,000 or more in an average-size store. You also save money on leasehold improvements because the walls, floors, ceilings, and lighting are already in place. You should not have to pay utility hookup fees which can range from a few to thousands of dollars. You may not need to buy construction permits or pay inspection fees, depending on the extent of your remodeling. You can also save money by updating some of the existing equipment rather than purchasing all new equipment.

While a coin laundry is under construction and producing no income, you must still pay rent, loan payments, insurance, taxes, and a variety of other expenses. This creates enormous pressure to finish construction, open the business, and build volume. An existing business, however, will generally be producing enough to cover these expenses. Your energies can instead be directed toward building upon an existing revenue base.

Coin Laundries — Road to Financial Independence

With all this in mind, you decide to buy an existing laundry. After weeks of driving back and forth across the city looking for the right location, you find the perfect area. There are thousands of potential customers and traffic patterns are perfect. There are a number of rundown laundries in the area, and they are all crowded on weekends. You decide to save a lot of money by cutting a good deal with one of the owners. You plan to remodel the store and capture the market. Your excitement level is high. The only way that you can get to sleep at night is by counting mountains of imaginary quarters.

Everything looks perfect except for one detail. After weeks of contacting laundry owners, not one will sell his business. Time to start looking for another area? Not if you're smart. There is obviously a need for a large, modern self-service laundry, and need is the key ingredient for success. The owners won't sell because they are making money! Now's the time to start thinking about where you are going to build a new store, starting from scratch.

It costs more to build a new store than to remodel an existing store, but this should <u>not</u> influence your decision to build if the location is good. The return on your investment should be the deciding factor. *The return from a new store in a good market will be better than from a remodeled laundry in a poor market. Remember, a good location is the single most important ingredient for the success of a self-service laundry.*

There are other considerations that will determine whether you remodel an existing store or build a new one. Even if there are coin laundries for sale, they may be priced much higher than their value. Many merchants boast that everything they own is for sale— at the right price! If you can't negotiate a reasonable price, then a new coin laundry is the only sensible solution.

What if the existing coin laundries are too small or lack enough equipment to accommodate customers during peak load times? If you can't acquire more space or add more equipment, consider building a new laundry that will satisfy market demand.

Does the laundry have enough parking? Don't underestimate the value of adequate parking. A new self-service laundry with

34

Buying versus Building

good parking will take customers from an established laundry with poor parking facilities—always! Without enough convenient parking spaces, a coin laundry will never achieve its potential volume.

Sometimes parking problems can be solved. When you are evaluating existing coin laundries, look for ways to add additional parking spaces or to make the existing spaces more convenient. You might provide access to a parking lot at the side or rear of the laundry by adding another entrance.

Inconvenient traffic flow may rule out an existing self-service laundry. Watch out for road dividers that don't allow customers to turn into the parking lot from their normal direction of travel, forcing them to drive many blocks out of their way. Carefully consider all inconveniences before deciding whether to buy or build.

Other factors may influence your decision to build a new self-service laundry rather than to buy an existing one. These include:

- Poor physical layout of existing store
- Poor exposure of existing store to prospective customers
- Intolerable landlord
- Restrictive lease
- Insufficient time left on lease
- Landlord unwilling to negotiate a new lease

The decision to build a new coin laundry or to buy an existing business is often a personal one. No formula applies because in many cases either decision would be correct from a business viewpoint. It is important, however, to thoroughly analyze both options using the guidelines described in this chapter before making your final decision.

Coin Laundries — Road to Financial Independence

To believe a business impossible is the way to make it so. How many feasible projects have miscarried through despondency, and been strangled in their birth by a cowardly imagination.

—Jeremy Collier

Destiny is not a matter of chance, it is a matter of choice; it is not a thing to be waited for, it is a thing to be achieved.

—William Jennings Bryan

6

EVALUATING
AN EXISTING
COIN LAUNDRY

B UYING AN ESTABLISHED coin laundry can be quite a challenge. The owner or business broker is almost certain to give you some "rule of thumb" to justify the selling price. This formula is usually based on gross revenue. Ignore this. The dollar value of a business is no more than a buyer is willing to pay. Base the value of the laundry on the following:

1. Value of assets
2. Profit
3. Return on investment
4. Lease terms (if space is leased)

VALUE OF ASSETS

The most common mistake made by inexperienced coin laundry buyers is overvaluing the equipment and leasehold improvements. The machines may be painted and waxed and looking good. But if they are old and worn out or use too much energy, they must be replaced. Replacement can cost many thousands of dollars!

Frequently, buyers purchase coin laundries based on what appears to be a good profit picture. Later they learn that a huge investment must be made to replace worn out equipment. The cost of the laundry including replacing some of the equipment is often higher than the cost of building an entirely new laundry with all new equipment!

Before a value can be placed on the equipment, you will need to know:

1. Age of the equipment
2. Life expectancy
3. Salvage value
4. Replacement cost
5. Present condition
6. Cost to recondition or repair
7. Cost to upgrade for energy efficiency

Equipment manufacturers and distributors can tell you the <u>age of the equipment</u> if you supply them with a list of model and serial numbers. Cross checking this information with both will eliminate errors and expose misleading statements. Other good sources of information are parts supply companies. Sometimes they too can tell the age of your equipment if you give them model and serial numbers.

If the seller is the original owner, you should be able to get a copy of the original purchase invoices for the equipment. If not, don't assume that the equipment isn't any older than the laundry. The owner may have purchased used equipment when the laundry was built.

<u>Life expectancy</u> of a particular brand and type of equipment is harder to determine. There is *actual* life expectancy and there is *practical* life expectancy. You are only interested in practical life expectancy. Some laundries have old, beat up, energy-wast-

Evaluating an Existing Coin Laundry

ing washers and dryers that need constant repair. The practical life expectancy of these machines may have ended 15 years ago.

Estimating practical life expectancy comes with experience, but initially you can draw on the experience of others. Talk with equipment manufacturers and distributors, parts supply companies, equipment service technicians, and experienced coin laundry operators. That will help you make a fairly accurate estimate of the practical life expectancy and salvage value for most equipment.

Replacement costs are easy. Get quotations from equipment manufacturers and distributors. Be sure to add freight, handling charges, and installation costs to get the total replacement cost for a machine. Some multi-store owners get firm quotations on new equipment, including written offers to buy the old equipment *before* purchasing the laundry.

If you are inexperienced in this industry, you will need help to determine the present condition of the equipment, the cost to recondition or repair it, and the cost to update it to make it energy efficient. Consider hiring a qualified consultant or a reputable service technician to act as one. If the equipment is maintained by an outside service firm, talk to the service technicians who work on the equipment. They can be a valuable source of information.

Equipment manufacturers and distributors are certainly able to provide this information, but remember that their main interest is to sell new equipment. This can influence their advice. They may also spread the news of your pending transaction, sparking the interest of other buyers and inflating the price.

Since many self-service laundry owners do their own maintenance and repair, ask to see their written maintenance schedules. Review these carefully. If a coin laundry owner cannot produce written maintenance schedules, it's likely that the equipment has been poorly maintained.

Place a dollar value on each item of equipment based on the number of years of useful life that remains. Set up a depreciation schedule on each type of equipment like the schedule shown on the following page.

MODEL 507 WASHERS

Year	Fractional Part	Depreciation	Asset Value
New			$750
1	1/7	$96.43	654
2	1/7	96.43	557
3	1/7	96.43	461
4	1/7	96.43	364
5	1/7	96.43	268
6	1/7	96.43	171
7	1/7	96.43	75 (Salvage)
		$675.00	

In this example, the practical life expectancy of a particular washer is seven years. At the end of this period, the washer could be sold to someone (like an owner of a small apartment house) for $75. The replacement cost of the washer is $750, including delivery and installation. The washer will decrease in value by $675 over the seven-year period or at the rate of $96.43 per year. If the age of the washer is five years, the dollar value would be established at $268. This is known as "straight-line" depreciation. It assumes that the value of the asset decreases by the same amount each year.

The cost to repair and maintain a machine increases with age. In addition, the appearance of the machine deteriorates at an increasing rate. This makes it less attractive to customers and, therefore, less valuable as an income-producing asset. A sliding scale depreciation rate known as the "sum-of-digits" method would give a more accurate value of the machine. The following page shows a sum-of-digits depreciation schedule for the same machine:

Evaluating an Existing Coin Laundry

MODEL 507 WASHERS

Year	Fractional Part	Depreciation	Asset Value
New			$750
1	7/28	$169	581
2	6/28	145	436
3	5/28	121	315
4	4/28	96	219
5	3/28	72	147
6	2/28	48	99
7	1/28	24	75 (Salvage)
28	28/28	$675	

The denominator (28) of the fractions used in the second column is found by adding the years in the first column. The other numbers (numerators) in the fractions are the numbers from the "year" column taken in reverse order.

The straight-line method provides a value of $268 for a five-year-old washer. The sum-of-digits method evaluates the same machine at $147, a difference of $121. Just who gets what portion of the $121 will depend on the condition and appearance of the machine and the negotiating skills of the buyer and seller. If the seller of the coin laundry is pricing the washer at $350, the washer would cost the buyer $137.50 ($350 - $75 ÷ 2) per year for the two remaining years of practical life. A new washer would cost only $96.43 per year based on straight-line depreciation.

Many self-service laundry owners are using old, outdated equipment. The equipment not only looks bad, but breaks down frequently and consumes too much energy. It's not unusual for an inexperienced buyer to pay $350 per washer for 15-year-old washers. Since the cost to rebuild each washer and update it for energy efficiency could easily be $300, you've paid $650 each for washers that are still unattractive to customers. You could have had new washers for $750! Because of the age, the actual market value of the rebuilt washers wouldn't be much higher than the $75 salvage value.

Be sure to judge the assets accurately. If the lease expires before the practical life of an asset is over and the landlord will not renew the lease, the asset must be sold. If the value of the asset was overestimated, you take a loss.

Let's see what can happen to an inexperienced buyer. Suppose a business broker shows you "the best deal in town" with a purchase price of "only $45,000." He tells you that the business generates $3,600 a month and to "grab it before it is sold." When you ask for details, he produces the following:

AVERAGE MONTHLY PROFIT

Gross Revenue $3,600

Expenses:
    Utilities $1,008
    Rent   600
    Insurance   200
    Repair   200
    Supplies   30
    Miscellaneous   100
    Total Expenses   2,138

Profit $1,462

He tells you that three full years remain on the lease, and because the landlord is a "good ol' boy," there should be no problem when it comes time to renew. "Suppose the lease is not renewed?" you ask. The broker tells you not to worry because you will still make over $52,000 in three years. In addition, all of that "valuable equipment" can be sold and part of the proceeds used to pay off the loan balance. Armed with this information, you put up $5,000 in cash and take out a $40,000 second mortgage on your home at 15 percent interest for 5 years. The monthly payments are $952, including principal and interest.

At the end of three years, the "good ol' boy" refuses to renew the lease and the equipment is sold as follows:

Washers	30	@	$75	=	$2,250
Dryers	15	@	$200	=	3,000
Miscellaneous					1,200
Total					$6,450

Your loan balance is $19,600 and there is your original investment of $5,000, all of which should be paid from the proceeds of the business. The average monthly cash intake was $1,462, of which $952 was paid to the lending institution each month as principal and interest. The following is a summary of what happened:

Cash from Business ($1,462 - $952 • 36 Months)		$18,360
Sale of Equipment		6,450
Total Cash		$24,810
Less Loan Balance	$19,600	
Less Original Investment	5,000	
Total Deductions		24,600
Amount Earned in 36 Months		$210

A total of $210 for three years of hard work and much risk is a terrible return! It would have been far better (and probably more fun) to have gambled with the $5,000 in Las Vegas. Inexperienced coin laundry buyers often find themselves in this situation. *Make sure this doesn't happen to you. Follow the steps outlined in this book.*

Much has been said about the value of the equipment, but what about the value of the leasehold improvements—the electrical wiring, plumbing, walls, ceiling, etc? When negotiating with a seller, keep this in mind:

- Leasehold improvements have no value beyond the life of the lease.
- Leasehold improvements have no value if the laundry is unprofitable.

It's impractical and often a violation of the lease to remove leasehold improvements. Therefore, they cannot be sold and will not contribute any cash if the lease expires or if you go out of business. This doesn't stop a seller from attaching some value to them, however, when setting the selling price of the laundry. If so, don't pay more for them than their depreciated value.

To determine the value of the leasehold improvements, use the same procedure that was used with the equipment. Set up a straight-line depreciation schedule. Since there is no salvage value, divide the original cost of the leasehold improvements by the number of months on the lease. This tells you how much the leasehold improvements should be depreciated for each month that they have been used. (Depreciation of leasehold improvements is covered in detail on page 187.)

When you purchase a coin laundry, you will usually find it necessary to upgrade or make additional improvements. Examine every nook and cranny to see what needs to be re-covered, painted, repaired, cleaned, rebuilt, thrown out, replaced or ignored. Make a list and estimate the cost of needed improvements. You can use this information to your advantage when negotiating with the seller.

PROFIT

Profit is what's left of the revenue after deducting expenses. A business owner is at the mercy of the buyer if the business is not making a profit. Since all business owners know this, they make

Evaluating an Existing Coin Laundry

every effort to show a good profit picture. When buying a coin laundry, you must verify the accuracy of the revenue figures and the expenses.

Many of the expenses can be determined by looking over the utility bills and the lease. It's harder to determine the revenue. Because a self-service laundry is a cash business, it's easy to cheat the government. Laundry owners who don't cheat may imply that they do when they produce monthly revenue statements, leading you to assume that the revenue is greater.

Estimating The Revenue

What can you do when the price of a laundry is based on the revenue it produces, yet the seller cannot document it to your satisfaction? Fortunately, you don't need to rely on the seller. You can determine the monthly revenue with reasonable accuracy from the water usage. If the seller cannot provide the water bills, then go directly to the water company. In some shopping centers the water used by the coin laundry is metered by the landlord. If so, ask the landlord for the figures.

Water usage is usually measured in cubic feet. Convert this to gallons by multiplying the cubic feet by 7.481 (gallons in a cubic foot). Divide the total monthly water consumption of the laundry (gallons) by the gallons of water used per washer during a cycle. This will provide the number of cycles that the washers ran during the month. Next, multiply the cycles by the price per wash to establish the total revenue that the washers produced during the month. The formula is as follows:

$$\frac{\text{Cubic Feet Of Water Used Per Month} \cdot \text{7.481 Gallons Per Cubic Foot}}{\text{Water Consumption Per Cycle}} \cdot \text{Price Charged Per Wash} = \text{Monthly Washer Revenue}$$

You may need to contact the manufacturer or equipment distributor to determine the water usage per cycle. You will need

Coin Laundries — Road to Financial Independence

to give them a model and serial number. These are found on a metal plate located somewhere on the washer cabinet (usually the rear).

Suppose a coin laundry has 28 top loading washers that use 34 gallons of water per cycle. The water bill tells you that the laundry used 18,952 cubic feet of water for the month. If the price is 75¢ per wash, the washers produced $3,127 in revenue during the month:

$$\frac{18,952 \cdot 7.481}{34} \quad \cdot \quad 75¢ \ = \ \$3,127$$

It's easy to determine the monthly revenue from the washers when all of the washers are the same model. If a laundry has different models of clothes washers, you can still make an accurate estimate, but it's a little more complicated. You will need to visit the laundry several times. The more visits you make, the greater the accuracy.

On each visit, make a note of the number of washers in operation—by model. Suppose that on your first visit there are 13 washers in operation: 8 single-load washers (type "A"), 2 triple-load washers (type "B"), and 3 double-load washers (type "C"). On your second visit, the figures are 14, 4 and 6. On your third visit, they are 18, 6 and 9. Use this information to figure out a percentage (of total water use) factor by washer type.

First, total the information from all three visits for each type of washer. Next, multiply these totals times the water consumption per cycle for each type of washer. Then determine the percentage use factor for each type of washer by dividing each result by the total water consumption. In other words, washer type "A" will use $^{1,360}/_{2,644}$ ths of the water, or 52 percent. Washer type "B" will use $^{564}/_{2,644}$ ths, or 21 percent, and so on. Use the chart on the following page as a model:

Evaluating an Existing Coin Laundry

Washer Type	Visit #1	Visit #2	Visit #3	Total All Visits	Gallons Water Per Cycle	Total Gallons	Projected Percentage Of Total Monthly Water Consumption By Washer Type
A	8	14	18	40	34	1,360	52%
B	2	4	6	12	47	564	21%
C	3	6	9	18	40	720	27%
						2,644	100%

Now that you have a percentage factor for each washer type, the rest is easy. First, multiply the percent factor times the monthly water usage for the laundry. This will give you the estimated monthly water usage for each type of washer. Next, divide this by the gallons used per cycle to get the number of cycles per month for each type of washer. Then multiply the number of cycles by the price per wash to get the monthly revenue produced by each type of washer as follows:

Washer Type	Use Factor	Total Gallons Of Water	Water Used Per Washer Type	Gallons Used Per Cycle	Cycles Per Month	Price Per Wash	Monthly Washer Revenue
A	52%	141,780	73,726	34	2,168	75¢	$1,626
B	21%	141,780	29,774	47	633	$2.50	$1,582
C	27%	141,780	38,280	40	957	$1.50	$1,435
	100%		141,780				$4,643

That takes care of the washers, but before you can determine the <u>total</u> revenue, you need to know the amount of revenue produced by the dryers. Again, on-site investigation is necessary. You have to find out the <u>average</u> amount of revenue produced when drying a load of clothes from each type of washer.

In other words, if you see a customer place three type "A" washer loads into a dryer and then deposit 4 quarters before removing the clothes, each load costs $33^{1}/3$¢ to dry. You may see another customer place three type "A" washer loads into another dryer and deposit 5 quarters before removing the clothes. Here, the cost to dry would be $41^{2}/3$¢ per type "A" washer load. Make several observations and record the results for each type of washer as follows:

Number Of Type "A" Washer Loads Placed In Dryer		Total Cost To Dry
3 Loads	————————	$1.00
3 Loads	————————	1.25
2 Loads	————————	.75
2 Loads	————————	.75
1 Load	————————	.50
11 Loads	————————	$4.25

Average Drying Revenue Per Type "A" Washer Load = 38.6¢
($4.25 ÷ 11 = 38.6¢)

The more you observe, the greater the accuracy. But don't get carried away. Too much dryer drum observation may cause your eyeballs to orbit.

Determine the average drying cost for each type of washer. Then calculate the monthly dryer revenue as follows:

Washer Type	Total Cycles Per Month	Average Revenue From Drying Each Washer Load	Total Monthly Dryer Revenue
A	2,168	38.6¢	$837
B	633	33.3¢	211
C	957	37.5¢	359
			$1,407

Evaluating an Existing Coin Laundry

Based on water usage, you find that the washers produced $4,643 in revenue and the dryers produced $1,407, for a total of $6,050 for the month. This is a fairly accurate estimate. If the seller shows revenue of $8,000 from the washers and dryers, ask him how he washes clothes without water. If the seller shows revenue of $4,000, he may not be reporting all the revenue. In this case, examine the figures carefully to determine the reason(s) for this large difference.

You can establish a sales history by analyzing past water bills. Investigate downward sales trends thoroughly to determine the reason(s) for the decline. A sharp drop in water consumption could mean that the owner purchased new energy saving washers. A gradual drop in water consumption most likely means that sales have decreased. <u>Find out why</u>!

What about other revenue, such as from services or vending machines? Check sales tickets to determine how much revenue is produced. Revenue produced by vending machines can be determined by checking invoices for the products being vended, such as laundry soap, soft drinks, candy, etc. Don't ever accept a verbal figure, especially if it includes a wink and a grin. Anyone who cheats the government may also try to cheat you.

Verify All Expenses

It's much easier to verify expenses because accurate records are usually kept for tax purposes. Ask the seller for a record of all expenses. Be sure to ask about any unusual expenses that may be incurred in the future, such as assessments for sewer, water, road improvements, etc. By law, sellers cannot knowingly withhold this information when asked. If they do and you suffer damages, you may have grounds for a lawsuit.

Use the following list of expenses as a guide when evaluating an existing coin laundry:

• Rent	• Utilities	• Wages
• Interest	• Taxes	• Telephone
• Advertising	• Insurance	• Attorney Fees

49

- Office Supplies
- Outside Services
- Accountant Fees
- Operating Supplies
- Maintenance and Repair

- Depreciation
- Sign Rental
- Annual Permits
- Inventory for Resale
- Security System or Service

There may be others. Check carefully before making a commitment.

The three major expenses are rent, wages (if there are employees), and utility costs. A copy of the lease will provide information on the rent and rent-related charges. Read the lease carefully. Some leases are 35 (or more) pages long and can contain a myriad of payments to the landlord.

Base rent is usually stated in dollars per square foot of space, payable monthly. There may also be a clause that increases the base rent from time to time. In some leases, the lessee is required to pay the landlord a percentage of the gross revenue above a predetermined amount. For example, a lease might specify quarterly payments of $6^{1}/_{2}$ percent of all revenue in excess of $25,000 during the quarter. These payments would be in addition to the monthly base rent.

Many leases allow the landlord to charge each store owner a portion of the expenses of maintaining and operating the shopping center. These expenses are usually divided among the store owners based on the percentage of the shopping center space that each store occupies. The following examples were taken from an actual lease:

- Management Fee
- Utility Room Charge
- Water
- Sewer Charge
- Trash Removal
- Sign Rental
- Parking Lot Lights

- Landscaping Charge
- Parking Lot Maintenance
- Security Service
- Sprinkler Service
- Real Estate Taxes
- Insurance

Evaluating an Existing Coin Laundry

As a rule, rent and all other charges specified in the lease should not exceed 25 percent of gross revenue. If they do, revenue must be increased or the rent decreased to bring this expense in line. Before making a commitment, be sure that you will be able to increase the revenue. If you are unsure, do not purchase the laundry until you renegotiate the lease. If you can't do either—walk away!

Most coin laundry expenses are fixed expenses—they remain the same whether the revenue increases or decreases. Utility expenses (water, natural gas, sewer and electricity) are variable expenses—they will vary with the amount of business. These expenses can be 40 percent (or more) of washer/dryer revenue in old laundries with outdated equipment. If the laundry has new machines, look for an average of 18 to 20 percent. Sometimes you can modify the old equipment to make it more energy efficient. This is covered in later chapters.

If the self-service laundry that you are considering has one or more employees, thoroughly analyze wages and related employee expenses. In addition to wages, you are required to pay a portion of the Social Security Tax, Worker's Compensation Insurance, and State and Federal Unemployment Taxes. Check carefully! There may be other taxes levied by the state, county, and city governments.

You will be required to withhold Federal Social Security Taxes, Federal Income Taxes, State Income Taxes (in some states), and the employee's portion of the Worker's Compensation Insurance premium from the employee's paycheck. Detailed employee records are required by law, so the seller will have this information. For additional information, study the "Employer's Tax Package." This package of tax laws and forms is available from the IRS and from the state, county, and city taxing authorities.

Depreciation is a major expense. In the long run, it will mean the difference between your success—or your failure. Although you are not paying out cash, the value of everything in a coin laundry decreases each month by a specific dollar amount. Sooner or later, you will have to pay that money to replace worn out equipment. Bad managers are often forced to sell their businesses when the equipment needs replacing.

Don't be "conned" by a seller. You may find later that you haven't made any money. Remember, you cannot determine how profitable an existing coin laundry is before you determine the depreciation and deduct it from the revenue. Set up depreciation schedules for all the equipment and leasehold improvements. Use the examples shown earlier in this chapter as a guide. (See chapter 15 for additional information on depreciation.)

The depreciation schedules used here are different from those established by the Internal Revenue Service. Federal depreciation schedules are based on an average of all brands and models of a broad classification of equipment. You have to use them when determining your tax liability. When you establish depreciation schedules for evaluating an existing coin laundry, you are basing them on the practical life expectancy of specific equipment. Don't use them when computing your tax liability.

There are other expenses. Interest on money used to build or buy a business is an expense. Laundry owners need operating supplies, including various cleaners, brushes, waxes, etc. Sometimes an owner will hire an outside service firm to clean carpets, windows, or to perform a daily janitorial service. If there are vending machines, a laundry owner must buy and maintain an inventory of soft drinks, candy bars, laundry soap, etc. Security systems and lighted exterior signs are sometimes leased on a monthly basis, rather than purchased outright. There can be taxes other than those associated with employees, such as business licenses, property taxes, sales taxes, etc. Be sure you uncover every expense. You want to put yourself in the best possible bargaining position.

Calculating Profit

Now that you have developed an accurate revenue pattern and documented all expenses, subtract the expenses from the revenue. The difference is profit, but you can't keep it all! If you borrow money to purchase a coin laundry, you will use part of the profit

Evaluating an Existing Coin Laundry

to pay back the loan principal. (Interest on the loan is an expense.) Part of the profit will be used to pay your income taxes. What's left is yours.

Review the "Estimated Profit Worksheet" below. Use it to estimate your profit and your net cash return when evaluating a possible acquisition. If you are not satisfied with the net profit, don't buy the business unless you are sure you are can increase the revenue, decrease the expenses, or do both.

The most obvious remedy for an unsatisfactory net profit is to offer less money for the business. This would reduce two major

---

ESTIMATED PROFIT WORKSHEET

Monthly Revenue:
    From Washers & Dryers $_____
    From Vending   _____
    Total Monthly Revenue $_____

Less Cost Of Vended Items   _____

Gross Profit $_____

Less Operating Expenses:
    Rent $_____
    Utilities   _____
    Depreciation   _____
    Interest On Loan   _____
    Maintenance & Repair   _____
    Operating Supplies   _____
    Insurance   _____
    Advertising   _____
    Taxes   _____
    Miscellaneous   _____
    Total Expenses   _____

Net Profit $_____
    Less Loan Principal   _____
    Less Estimated Income Taxes   _____
    Total Paid Out From Profit Each Month   _____

Net Cash To Owner Each Month $_____

expenses: depreciation, and interest on the money you borrow to purchase your business. This would also provide you with more cash. You would be paying smaller loan payments to the lending institution out of each month's profit.

RETURN ON INVESTMENT

The question most often asked by people who have money to invest is: "What is the return on my investment?" Investors use this information as a measuring tool to compare one investment opportunity with another. They also consider the risk factor that is associated with each.

If you put $20,000 into a savings account, you might receive a 5-percent ($1,000) annual return on your money. There would be very little risk and no expenditure of your time or energy. The same $20,000 could be used to purchase a small self-service laundry that would produce $1,000 in cash for you every month—a 60-percent annual return on your $20,000 investment. But there is a trade-off for the higher return: a much greater risk of losing your $20,000. Besides this, you are going to spend a lot of time and energy running a self-service laundry. It's the old economic principle: "Somethin' for nothin' ain't."

Inexperienced entrepreneurs often base their buying decisions on how much they have to borrow to buy a business rather than the return on their investment. Avoid this mistake. Use the Estimated Profit Worksheet to determine whether you can afford to purchase a business. It will tell you if there is ample cash left over to satisfy your needs and to act as a safety net against your mistakes. An experienced multi-store owner might operate a new store on a small cash margin, but the inexperienced would be wise to have a good cash return.

TERMS OF THE LEASE

Before purchasing a coin laundry, make sure you are thoroughly familiar with all of the terms and conditions of the lease.

Evaluating an Existing Coin Laundry

Do you fully understand all the expenses that you will be paying relative to the lease? Do you know your rights?—your obligations? Put all communications with the seller and the landlord in writing, but only after approval by your attorney. Good written communication can do much to eliminate confusion and misunderstanding which often leads to poor tenant-landlord relations.

The lease must have ample time left if you are to realize a good return on your investment. If not, renegotiate the lease before purchasing the business. Laundry owners have been evicted by their landlords after purchasing coin laundries with expired leases. If the lease is expired (or almost expired), the seller has nothing to sell except a lot of used equipment which happens to be stored in a space that was once a self-service laundry.

There are sharp business people who are constantly on the prowl for expired coin laundry leases. In one instance, a laundry owner tried to sell his business for $45,000. The prospective buyer strung him along until the lease expired, and then he negotiated a new lease directly with the landlord. As a condition of the previous lease, the landlord owned all the leasehold improvements, which he gave to the new owner. The new owner was eventually able to buy the equipment from the previous owner for less than $2,000, a savings of $43,000. Profit was increased by 57 percent within nine months. The new owner calculated the return on his investment to be 660 percent!

Opportunities as good as this one are not easy to find. Take the time to become familiar with all the coin laundries in the market. Look for those that are rundown and unprofitable. Find out if the landlord is dissatisfied with the lessee and how much time is left on the lease. Be patient, but be persistent. You can usually turn up a good business opportunity, particularly in a metropolitan area.

Check with local government agencies before assuming a lease. Are there any recent or pending zone changes in the area? Are there any road building or improvement plans that might affect your laundry? Are there any property easements? If so, what is the potential effect on your business? Check the building permits in your marketing area. Are there any permits for competitive coin laundries or shopping centers that might contain a self-service laundry? Remember, a new shopping center will change consumer habits and shopping patterns. If your location were annexed by another municipality, how would this affect your business?

Be a good negotiator when buying your business. Leverage your negotiations with the seller by making sure he knows, beyond any doubt, that you intend to own a self-service laundry in the area. Make the seller understand that if you cannot purchase his laundry at the right price, you will build a new one. He will understand that this will make his business unprofitable.

Be careful when negotiating with several coin laundry owners. It's easy to become confused. Carefully evaluate each offer or counteroffer to see how it will affect the return on your investment. If you don't, chances are you will pay too much.

All good negotiators have one thing in common—patience. Don't become too intense. Stay loose! Much of what is wrong with management in America today is the lack of patience, a willingness to sacrifice long-term gain for short-term results. Don't let this happen to you.

7

SURVEYING
THE MARKET

BUYING A COIN laundry or starting a new one before you survey your market is like drilling an oil well without doing a geological survey. This is gambling, and gambling is risky! Smart investors don't gamble with their money. Take time to thoroughly survey your market. It's a small sacrifice to make to guarantee your success.

You have many important management decisions to make when buying or starting a business. Many of these decisions cannot be altered once you act without suffering huge financial losses. That's why it is important to base your decisions on facts, not conjecture. A survey of your market will provide the facts you need to ensure your success.

WHAT YOU NEED TO KNOW

A business cannot be successful without customers. You need to know yours intimately <u>before</u> you spend any money or make any commitments. Don't hire contractors, purchase equipment, or sign a lease before you have answers to these questions:

- Who are your prospective customers?
- What are their needs?
- When will they be in need of your product or service?
- Where are they presently getting the product or service?
- Why should they do business with you?

You will decide the size of your store based on the answers to these questions. This information will guide you when you select and purchase your equipment. It will influence your pricing and your business hours. Your business will grow faster if you develop your advertising program based on the information from your survey. It will also get better results with fewer advertising dollars.

THE PROSPECTIVE CUSTOMER DATA SHEET

There is no substitute for one-on-one contact when looking for prospective customers. The question is: Would you personally knock on doors and visit with prospective customers until you filled out 500 questionnaires? You're not excited about that? OK, let's try another question. Would you do it to keep from losing $100,000? Sure! What if it would help make you a millionaire? You bet you would!

You can become a millionaire by owning and operating profitable coin laundries. You make them profitable by good planning and eliminating costly mistakes. This is the purpose of your market survey—to help you do both. Use the "Prospective Customer Data Sheet" on the following page to record information from your survey. Locate as many prospects as you can and fill out a Prospective Customer Data Sheet on each. The more the better!

If the Prospective Customer Data Sheet is so important, why isn't it more detailed? Too much detail defeats its purpose. Most people don't like answering a lot of questions, particularly per-

Surveying the Market

PROSPECTIVE CUSTOMER DATA SHEET

Name_____ Street Address_____

Telephone Number_____ Family Size_____
                                                                (number of people)

Presently doing laundry at:

☐ self-service coin laundry_____
                                          (name)

☐ apartment house laundry   ☐ parent or friend

☐ other_____
                                (describe)

Most convenient day for doing laundry_____ Time_____

Washing machine preference:

☐ top loader   ☐ single-load front loader

☐ double-load front loader   ☐ triple-load front loader

Dryer preference:

☐ multi-load dryer   ☐ single-load dryer

Most frequently shopped grocery store:

Name_____ Location_____

If using a central laundry room or self-service coin laundry, what is

your biggest complaint?_____

_____

sonal ones. They especially don't like filling out long question-naires. Keep it short. Don't antagonize prospective customers.

GETTING INFORMATION

Walking is good exercise. Get used to it. You cannot survey your market by driving around in your automobile. Go to where your prospective customers live, visit them and find out where they are washing their clothes. Then visit each laundry facility.

Don't hire someone to do this for you unless you are physi-cally unable to do it yourself. You cannot fully understand or "get the feel" for your market by trying to see it through the eyes of others. A good market survey takes good judgment. Someone else won't necessarily have the good judgment you do.

Spend the time to survey your entire market. Personally visit and inspect:

- All multi-family housing units
- Many single-family homes
- All motels
- All competitive laundries.

Multi-Family Housing

Many of your prospective customers will live in apartments. Become familiar with every apartment complex in your market. Each will fall into one of four categories:

1. No central laundry facilities in the complex. No washer or dryer hookups in the apartments.
2. A central laundry facility in the complex. No washer or dryer hookups in the apartments.
3. Individual washer and dryer hookups in every apartment. No central laundry facility in the apartment complex.
4. Individual washer and dryer hookups in every apartment. A central laundry facility in the apartment complex.

Surveying the Market

Experienced coin laundry owners get excited when they find an apartment complex without central laundry facilities or individual washer/dryer hook-ups in the apartments. This makes every tenant in the apartment complex a prospective customer. When you find this situation, fill out a Prospective Customer Data Sheet for every tenant.

What if the individual apartments have laundry hookups, but there are no central laundry facilities in the apartment complex? Survey every apartment. Find the tenants that do not own washers and/or dryers. Fill out a Prospective Customer Data Sheet on each.

What if the apartment complex has a central laundry facility? The tenants may be prospects for your laundry if the central laundry facility doesn't meet their needs. Study it carefully. Talk with the tenants. Then fill out a Prospective Customer Data Sheet for every tenant if you find that any of the following conditions exist:

- Washing or drying prices are too high.
- Laundry room hours are inconvenient.
- The laundry room is dirty and/or poorly lit.
- The equipment is old and poorly maintained.
- Problems exist with theft of tenants' clothes from laundry room.
- There are insufficient washers and dryers to meet tenants' needs.

Be sure to determine the actual cost to wash and dry a load of clothes. The coin slide on a single-load dryer may take two quarters—50¢. This doesn't mean that you can dry a load of clothes for 50¢. The dryer may require $1.00 to dry a load. In some cases, the tenants may be paying $1.50 to dry a large load of blue jeans or towels.

Even if the tenants can dry a load of clothes for 50¢, they may still be prospects for a self-service laundry. They may prefer to use a self-service laundry that has triple-load dryers. There, they can dry 3 loads for $1.00—and do it faster.

Coin Laundries — Road to Financial Independence

Double or triple-load washers are normally not available in the central laundry facilities at apartment complexes. Visit with the tenants and learn their preferences. Those who prefer to use large-load washers are prospects for a self-service laundry. Fill out a Prospective Customer Data Sheet on each.

Single-Family Homes

It is too time consuming and impractical to contact every single-family home in your market. Pick neighborhoods with the least expensive single-family homes, where the residents are more likely to be self-service laundry prospects. Personally visit as many of these homes as you can. Fill out Prospective Customer Data Sheets for residents who don't have washers and/or dryers.

What about residents of more affluent neighborhoods? While some of those residents need to use self-service laundries, you don't have time to visit every single-family dwelling. Use a mailing service or door-hanger advertising company to distribute your Prospective Customer Data Sheets. The cost is usually very reasonable because you share the distribution expense with other businesses.

Have your Prospective Customer Data Sheets printed on a return-address, postage-paid card. The cards should be accompanied by a letter explaining that you are planning to build (or remodel) a self-service laundry in the area, and your plans will be based on their advice.

Encourage prospects to fill out and return the Prospective Customer Data Sheets by promising to mail them free coupons for washing and drying at your new coin laundry. Drawings for prizes can also be used as an effective inducement if they are legal in your area.

Motels

Don't overlook the local motels and the "bed-and-breakfast" lodgings since travelers are often in need of laundry facilities. Be sure to keep them supplied with your literature and advertising material. You will also want to establish a good relationship with the owners and managers of these businesses because they may need to use your large-load washers to launder bedspreads, throw-rugs and other large items.

Competitive Laundries

Visit every competitive laundry in your market. Determine the amount of business that each is doing, using the methods described on pages 45 through 49. Total the figures. This will tell you how much self-service laundry business is presently being done in your market. Use this information when you estimate the amount of revenue you can expect your laundry to produce.

Why go to the trouble of visiting apartments and single-family homes when you could limit your market survey to competitive laundries? Any prospect for your laundry is already using your competitors' laundries, right? WRONG! Many of your prospective customers are not using the self-service laundries in your market.

If the local self-service laundries are rundown and dirty, many tenants will continue to use the central laundry facilities in their apartment complex. It's more convenient. Others are willing to drive great distances to use clean, modern self-service laundries when they are not available nearby. Remember, a major reason for surveying your market is to learn the needs of your prospective customers. You must meet those needs to get their business.

HOW TO USE INFORMATION FROM YOUR SURVEY

The market survey will tell you what you need to know to estimate the monthly revenue from your new self-service laundry. Monthly revenue, in turn, will determine the size of your store and the amount of equipment you will need. You must estimate your revenue before you can develop your operating plan or apply for financing.

You will visit all competitive laundries when you survey your market, including self-service laundries and central laundry facilities in multi-family housing. You will learn what is being charged to wash and dry a load of clothes. This information will influence your pricing.

The Prospective Customer Data Sheets tell you what type of laundry equipment your prospects prefer. They list the day and hour that they do their laundry. This information will influence the type of equipment you purchase and your business hours. Remember, if you want to turn prospects into customers, you must meet their needs.

It can take months and sometimes years for a new business to reach the break-even point, where revenue equals expenses. Meanwhile, you pay the expenses. You must also pay back part of your loan each month. Advertising to a list of prospective customers will make your business grow faster with fewer advertising dollars. It will also reduce the amount of time it takes to break even, saving you many thousands of dollars.

The Prospective Customer Data Sheets show where your prospective customers are buying their groceries. Since this information is valuable to a grocery store manager, visit the manager of the store nearest to you and suggest a joint advertising program. Some grocery store managers will pay 100 percent of the cost of the program if you supply the list. You will gain customers and reduce your advertising costs at the same time.

ESTIMATING YOUR MONTHLY REVENUE

Since your monthly revenue estimate will be the basis for many important financial decisions, it must be accurate. Your market survey will allow you to make two separate estimates from two different sets of figures. You can then compare the figures for accuracy.

Using Information From Prospective Customer Data Sheets
Let's assume that your market survey produced a total of 505 Prospective Customer Data Sheets. Each sheet lists the number of

people in the family. Separate the prospects into five groups according the following classifications:

Customer Classification		Average Washer Loads Per Week
College Students	——————————	1/2 To 1 Load
Elderly	——————————	1/2 To 1 Load
Singles	——————————	1 To 2 Loads
Couples Without Children	——————————	2 To 3 Loads
Families With Children	——————————	3 To 5 Loads (Or More)

The next step is to estimate the number of single-load washer loads these prospects launder each week. The following estimate uses an average of 4 loads for a family, 2 loads for couples, $1\frac{1}{2}$ loads for singles, and $\frac{3}{4}$ of a load for the elderly:

Estimated Sales Volume

310	Families	•	4 Loads Average	=	1,240	Loads Per Week
85	Couples	•	2 Loads Average	=	170	Loads Per Week
37	Singles	•	1-1/2 Loads Average	=	55	Loads Per Week
45	Elderly	•	3/4 Loads Average	=	34	Loads Per Week
	Total			=	1,499	Loads Per Week

If your average price for a washed and dried load of clothes is $1.25, your average monthly sales volume will be $8,057 (1,499 loads per week • $1.25 per load • 4.3 weeks per month).

Using Information From A Survey Of Competitive Laundries

Estimate the sales volume of each competitive coin laundry using the method described on pages 45 through 49:

Dollar Volume of Competitive Laundries

Competitor A	——————————	$4,500 Per Month
Competitor B	——————————	$5,600 Per Month
Competitor C	——————————	$7,667 Per Month

Coin Laundries — Road to Financial Independence

Next, estimate the percentage of business you expect to gain from each competitive coin laundry as follows:

Estimated Customer Capture from Competitive Laundries

40 Percent Of Laundry A	———————————	$1,800
20 Percent Of Laundry B	———————————	1,120
30 Percent Of Laundry C	———————————	2,300
Other (Apartments, Homes,Transient, Etc.)	————	2,100
Total	———————————	$7,320

It's not easy to estimate the percentage of business that you will take from your competition. It's more of a "guesstimate." Just give it your best shot. Remember, your laundry will attract customers because:

- It's new and modern.
- It's clean.
- It has convenient parking.
- It's more accessible.
- Etc.

Now compare both estimates. Don't substitute one for the other. You need to consider <u>both</u> for the sake of accuracy.

Later you will learn how to use this information to plan and develop a profitable self-service laundry. The next chapter shows you how to determine the size of your laundry based on the information from your market survey.

8

PLANNING THE SIZE OF YOUR STORE

THERE IS A TENDENCY for the inexperienced to overbuild a new coin laundry. Their excitement level is up, so they are vulnerable to high-pressure sales tactics by equipment manufacturers and distributors. But beware! When a coin laundry is too large for its market, you can suffer huge financial losses, or even face bankruptcy.

The days of inexpensive store space are gone forever. This fact makes rent one of your three biggest expenses. Carefully consider how much space you will need to operate. This decision is important because it will have a significant influence on your profit. Plan your needs carefully before signing a lease.

It's better to undersize than to oversize your laundry. If your laundry cannot handle market demand, you will still make a substantial profit. And you can always build another coin laundry in the same area. On the other hand, a coin laundry that is too large for the market will be a tremendous drain on your finances.

Coin Laundries — Road to Financial Independence

Let's look at an example. Suppose you rented 2,000 square feet of space at 92¢ per square foot per month. You prepare the space for the equipment and install 38 washers and 19 dryers. Later you learn that a laundry with 24 washers and 12 dryers requiring only 1,200 square feet of space would satisfy consumer demand. The following shows how much you'd be spending unnecessarily:

EXCESS EXPENSES FROM OVERSIZED LAUNDRY

Excess Rent Expense	—	$736.00
Excess Depreciation Expense	—	194.17
Excess Interest Expense	—	99.40
Total Excess Expenses Per Month	—	$1,029.57

Here's how you arrive at these figures:

RENT: You have a total of 800 square feet of excess space (2,000 - 1,200 = 800) that costs 92¢ per square foot per month. The total excess rent expense is $736.00 per month (800 • 92¢ = $736.00).

DEPRECIATION: If your washers cost $750 each, and have a practical life expectancy of 7 years (84 months) with a $75 salvage value, the straight line depreciation for 14 washers would be $112.50 per month ($750 - $75 ÷ 84 months • 14 washers).
If your dryers cost $1,600 each, and have a practical life expectancy of 10 years (120 months) with a $200 salvage value, the straight line depreciation for 7 dryers would be $81.67 per month ($1,600 - $200 ÷ 120 months • 7 dryers). Total monthly depreciation expense for 14 excess washers and 7 excess dryers would be $194.17.

Planning the Size of Your Store

INTEREST: Fourteen washers that cost $750 each, and 7 dryers that cost $1,600 each, would add $21,700 to your debt. The average monthly interest paid on a 5-year loan for $21,700 at 10 percent is $99.40.

In short, if you built a 38 washer coin laundry in a market that would only support one with 24 washers, you'd pay $1,029.57 a month in excess rent, depreciation, and interest. You would also waste a lot of capital on excess plumbing, wiring, lighting, and other leasehold improvements. You would pay extra for an over-sized water heater plus additional monthly costs to operate it. Think of the money you'd waste on utility hookup charges! You would also be faced with excess costs for heating or air conditioning, cleaning, and maintenance. *This is a heavy price to pay for an inadequate market survey!*

It takes know-how to estimate the amount of space you need for a self-service laundry. Fortunately, you can learn by studying other self-service laundries. Develop an eye for detail and use your common sense. Look for these things when visiting self-service laundries:

1. Size of space
2. Number and type of washers
3. Number and type of dryers
4. Layout
5. Wasted space

Don't try to measure everything. If you do, you will disrupt the business and aggravate the laundry owner. Estimate dimensions by using floor tiles or 2-foot by 4-foot ceiling panels as a reference. Determine the size of the laundry, aisle widths, and other dimensions. Use this information to sketch store layouts. You can then study them to see how they can be improved and how you might eliminate wasted space.

The more stores you analyze, the more informed you will be. It doesn't take long before you can develop some very good store layouts. You will become proficient in the use of space. Show your plans to equipment manufacturers, equipment distributors, or consultants for their input. In the final analysis, however, your best judgment should prevail when planning your laundry.

The amount of space that you will need will depend on several interacting factors:

- Equipment
- Equipment-use-factor
- Business volume
- Load-spread
- Attended or unattended laundry
- Services offered

EQUIPMENT

The type and amount of equipment you choose will influence how much space you need. You need less space for 24 top-loading washers than for 24 high-extract-speed front-loading washers. Top-loading washers placed back-to-back are separated by only six-to-eight inches. Since they are not bolted to the floor, you can pull them forward into the aisle for service. Front-loading washers with high spin-speeds are normally bolted to the floor and are not moved during service or maintenance. Many brands of front-loaders will require two or more feet of space behind the washer for service or maintenance.

Top-loading washers can easily save you 50 square feet of space over front-loading washers in a 24-washer store. If you select stacked dryers over some models of 30-pound-capacity dryers, you could save an additional 190 square feet. Your total space savings would be 240 square feet. At 92¢ per square-foot per month for rent, your total savings would be $220 per month. Saving space, however, is not your only consideration when selecting equipment as you will learn in Chapter 10.

Planning the Size of Your Store

EQUIPMENT-USE-FACTOR

The equipment-use-factor, based on the washers, is the percentage of available cycles that the washers average daily. In other words, if a washer cycle is 32 minutes and the average user requires 5 minutes to load and unload the machine, theoretically the washer could run 24.3 cycles in a 15 hour day (15 hours • 60 minutes ÷ 37 minutes = 24.3). If all washers are used an average of 5 times per day, the equipment-use-factor is 20.5 percent (5 ÷ 24.3).

The expected use-factor will influence the amount of equipment you need which, in turn, will influence the amount of space you need. Most laundries have an equipment-use-factor of between 8 and 33 percent. Most new laundries are designed for an equipment-use-factor of between 22 and 26 percent. Based on a 14-hour day and a 7-day week, this is between 5 and 6 cycles per day for each washer.

BUSINESS VOLUME

You make the most profit when you size your store to handle the business volume you expect. If your store is too big for the market, your excess expenses will decrease your profit. If your store is too small, you lose the opportunity to make a bigger profit. This is where your market survey will prove invaluable. It will give you all the information you need to estimate your business volume.

LOAD-SPREAD

If you could operate at capacity all the time, you would become very rich very fast! This would be a 100 percent equipment-use-factor. Unfortunately, customers don't present themselves in a steady stream from the time you open until you close. There are many idle hours.

A laundry that does 80 percent of its business on weekends is said to have an <u>uneven</u> load-spread, while a laundry whose business volume is steady throughout the entire week is said to have a <u>uniform</u> load-spread.

Load-spread influences the equipment use-factor which influences the amount of equipment you need to handle the volume. This influences the size of your store. A more uniform load-spread means that less equipment is needed to meet market demand.

From a cost standpoint, you would be better off owning a laundry with 24 washers running at a 28.8-percent equipment-use-factor producing $5,082 in revenue per month than one with 32 washers operating at a 21.6-percent equipment-use-factor producing the same $5,082 in revenue. But if you have an uneven load-spread, 24 washers may not satisfy market demand.

For example, what if your market has only one major employer and the employees all work the same hours? Your laundry could get most of its customers on the weekends, leaving much of your equipment idle Monday through Friday. If your market has many employers, chances are that the hours of employment would vary considerably. As a result, you would have a more even load-spread throughout the week. You would require fewer machines and less space to obtain the same dollar volume.

What about a coin laundry in a resort area? Business is seasonal in many resort towns. You would need to plan a self-service laundry that would handle market demand during the three or four months of the peak tourist season. Your laundry would have considerable idle capacity the rest of the year.

Sometimes you can improve your load-spread by reducing your price during days that are consistently slow. Many of your customers will change the day they do their laundry to take advantage of the price reduction. Your overall business will increase because your laundry will not be as crowded, and fewer customers will be turned away.

Planning the Size of Your Store

ATTENDED OR UNATTENDED STORE

Attended self-service laundries require more space. The amount of additional space you need will depend on the services that you plan to offer. At the very least, you should add a rest room for your attendant. The law requires this in some areas.

SERVICES OFFERED

Plan your space needs around the services that you plan to offer. For instance, if you are going to offer a wash-and-fold service, you will need space for a counter. This type of service also requires plenty of clothes-storage space and space for sorting, folding, and packaging. If you are planning for a large wash-and-fold business, you will need to install additional washers and dryers behind the counter to be used only by the attendant.

There is no hard and fast rule for determining the amount of space you will need. Use good judgment and common sense. Rely on the Prospective Customer Data Sheets discussed in Chapter 7. They provide you with the day and time that potential customers prefer to do their laundry (load-spread), as well as the equipment they prefer.

CALCULATING YOUR SPACE REQUIREMENTS

In Chapter 7 you learned how to estimate washer loads based on information from the Prospective Customer Data Sheets. Suppose your Prospective Customer Data Sheets show that consumer demand is about 4,300 loads per month with a fairly even load-spread. If the majority of your prospects prefer top-loading washers and stacked dryers, you would estimate your equipment needs as follows:

$$\frac{4,300 \text{ Loads per Month}}{30 \text{ Days per Month}} = 144 \text{ Loads per Day}$$

73

Coin Laundries — Road to Financial Independence

$$\frac{144 \text{ Loads per Day}}{6 \text{ Cycles per Machine per Day}} = 24 \text{ Washers}$$

As you can see, you will need 24 washers and 12 stacked dryers (24 drying chambers) to satisfy market demand. With an even load-spread, you could get six cycles per day from your washers. This would be an equipment-use-factor of approximately 25 percent, which is a good goal to work toward.

In addition to washers and dryers, your coin-operated laundry will require a water heater, a coin and bill changer, clothes-folding tables, a soap vending machine, and seating. You will need a small amount of additional space if you plan on vending machines for coffee, soft drinks, candy, or food. Game machines would also add to your space needs. A lounge area with tables and seating would mean even more needed space.

By now you will know a lot from studying other self-service laundries. You will know how much space is needed for a coin laundry with 24 top-loading washers and 12 stacked dryers, including the necessary peripheral equipment. This will range from 875 to 1,400 square feet, depending on the services that you plan to offer.

Experienced self-service laundry owners try to keep their total rent expense below 25 percent of the total revenue from their washers and dryers. You would be wise to do the same unless you expect a significant portion of your profit to come from services or other businesses that you plan to operate from the same space.

Suppose you determine that consumer demand is 4,300 loads per month. If your average price is $1.25 per washed and dried load, your total monthly revenue from the washers and dryers would be $5,375. This means that your rent should not be more than $1,344 per month.

$$25\% \cdot \$5,375 \text{ (Monthly Revenue)} = \$1,344 \text{ (Maximum Monthly Rent Allowance)}$$

Planning the Size of Your Store

What if rent and rent-related expenses total 92¢ per square foot per month for the space you are considering? In this case, limit your space to a maximum of 1,461 square feet:

$$\frac{\$1,344 \text{ (Maximum Rent per Month)}}{92¢ \text{ per Square Foot Cost}} = 1,461 \text{ Square Feet}$$

You should have no problem installing 24 washers and 12 stacked dryers in 1,461 square feet of space. You could even have a lounge area with vending machines and a variety of services. Suppose you don't want an attended coin laundry. If you build a 24-washer laundry that will do the same volume in 950 square feet of space, you will save $470 per month in rent. The $470 savings is pure profit. Get the idea?

Business without profit is not business any more than a pickle is candy.

—Charles Frederick Abbott

To get profit without risk, experience without danger, and reward without work, is as impossible as it is to live without being born.

—A. P. Gouthey

9

UTILITY HOOKUP
AND USE CHARGES

IMAGINE WHAT IT would be like to build and operate a self-service laundry in a country where the government had the power to make its own rules and change them at will. Suppose some bureaucrat set an arbitrary fee of $1,000 per washer (payable in cash) before you were allowed to begin business. This fee could easily be a quarter of the total cost to build your laundry! If this shocks you, read on, because this situation exists in many parts of the United States. <u>Do not sign a lease before you verify all utility hookup and use charges in your area!</u>

Utility hookup fees can be substantial—as much as $1,000 or more to hook into the sewer for every clothes washer in your coin laundry. This does not include the cost for labor or materials. In other words, you have to pay $24,000 plus the cost of the hookup for a 24-washer store. That's not all! You must also pay a monthly charge for using the sewer.

The cost of a water tap (the one-time cost to hook into the main water line) could be equally as high. In some parts of this country, ranchers are still getting shot over water rights. Coin laundry owners must pay $20,000 to $30,000 in water hookup fees for the same reason—water scarcity.

BE CAUTIOUS! Unscrupulous equipment distributors sometimes recommend locations and sell equipment to prospective laundry owners without informing them about the utility hookup fee requirements. *If you don't learn about the fees until after you sign the lease, you could lose a lot of money.*

Don't be mislead by government bureaus or agencies. Their representatives have told store owners that there were no fees when there were! It pays to check and check again. Talk with every department or agency on the city, county, and state level that has anything to do with water or sewer services.

It's best to get information in writing when dealing with government employees, only because a written statement is more likely to be accurate than a verbal one. But don't expect to hold the government financially accountable if its employee gives incorrect information. It's always the private sector who suffers the financial losses caused by inept government employees.

NEGOTIATING FEES WITH THE GOVERNMENT

Not all fees or charges are carved in stone. It's worth a try to get these reduced. First, find out who has the authority to change the regulations. Next, through a process of informational give-and-take, set the stage for good negotiations with that individual. A reasonable compromise can often be reached.

You may find that the water and sewer charges were established when top-loading washers used up to 63 gallons of water per cycle. This situation has changed considerably since the energy crunch. Today, most top-loading washers use only 34 gallons per cycle. Front-loading washers use even less water to wash the same amount of clothes. Because modern coin laundries need less than half of the water that they did in the past, they are easier on the sewer system. Use this information as a basis for your negotiations.

Sewer agencies may not realize that the water used by a coin laundry is not all discharged to the sewer. Some of it is evaporated by the dryers. A normal 8-pound washer load will weigh 15 pounds or more after washing. This means that 7 pounds of water (approximately .833 gallons) is evaporated in the clothes dryer. In other words, 2.6 percent of the water never enters the sewer.

Government employees are not experts on self-service laundries. Most know little about utility requirements. Many are surprised to learn that the equipment-use-factor is only 22-to 26-percent, not 50-to 75-percent. If you are going to get the fees reduced, you must educate that government employee. If a satisfactory compromise cannot be reached, you can always solicit the support of your elected officials.

You have nothing to lose and everything to gain by being creative in your negotiations. One laundry owner was able to persuade the sewer agency to waive the hookup fees for his new store after closing an old coin laundry located in the same block. He convinced the agency that the new store would make fewer demands on the existing sewer system.

NEGOTIATING FEES WITH THE LANDLORD

Don't stop your negotiations here. When you negotiate the lease, try to get your landlord to pay all (or part) of the utility hookup fees. The ideal situation is to have your landlord provide all the utility services (according to your specifications) to the interior of your space and pay all the government fees, too.

A shopping center owner is required to pay utility hookup fees when the shopping center is under construction. When your center was built, the payments may have been sufficient to cover part (if not all) of the charges levied against your self-service laundry. *Don't assume that the landlord is aware of this.* Few landlords know all government procedures and regulations. You will have to do the leg-work and the research. It's worth it. You could save yourself a lot of money.

Investigate thoroughly and negotiate skillfully. You may save thousands upon thousands of dollars. But what if you fail to reduce these fees? Don't let this stand in your way if the coin laundry will provide you with a <u>good</u> return on your investment. After all, your main concern is to make money—isn't it?

10

SELECTING
YOUR EQUIPMENT

TEN DIFFERENT LAUNDRY owners are likely to have ten different opinions on the best equipment for a self-service laundry. Opinions are often based solely on personal preference. Base your decisions on facts, not opinions.

The cost of your equipment will run from 60 to 80 percent of the total cost of your new laundry. This is a major expense. You must select your equipment carefully if you are to get the maximum return on your investment. Below is a list of the important issues when comparing equipment:

- Cost
- Practical Life Expectancy
- Cost-To-Revenue Ratio
- Energy Efficiency
- Customer Preference
- Durability
- Service And Repair

- Warranty
- Cost And Availability Of Parts
- Safety
- Manufacturer And Distributor Assistance

These guidelines will help you compare equipment.

COST

The most frequently asked question is, "What does it cost?" What you really should be asking is, "What is the cost?" When comparing the cost of equipment, you need to know the following:

- Cost of the machine
- Freight and handling charges
- Installation cost

Freight and handling charges must be treated as part of the cost of a machine. This is important when comparing prices on the same model from several different sources. You may save $25 per washer with one distributor, but what do you gain if you have to pay $30 more for shipping it?

Installation costs vary considerably for different types of equipment. This is especially true for washers. Top-loading washers do not have to be bolted to the floor. They can sit on almost any type of floor, from wood to concrete. The drain hose is put into the standpipe, the cord is plugged into a 120-volt outlet, and the water hoses are screwed onto the water valves. You're ready to go!

On the other hand, a large front-loading washer may require a 12-inch reinforced concrete subfloor, plus a reinforced concrete mounting pad. The washer base is then grouted and bolted onto the mounting pad. Part of the concrete floor must be removed and a floor sink installed to handle the drain water. High-pressure water

Selecting Your Equipment

pipe is then connected directly to the washer, and three-phase, 240-volt power is wired into the machine.

As you might expect, there is a considerable difference in installation costs between a top-loading washer and a large front-loading one, but there are other factors to consider. The practical life expectancy of the front-loading washer could be 15 years longer than the top-loader. Be sure you consider all factors when selecting your equipment.

Contact the manufacturers and/or distributors of the equipment you are considering. Ask for a set of installation specifications and diagrams. Study them carefully. Use the following checklist as a guide when gathering information on your washers and dryers:

Washers

- Floor or subfloor requirements
- Base mounting specifications
- Sewer connection details
- Water line size and pressure requirements
- Voltage, amperage, and phase requirements
- Maintenance access requirements
- Space requirements

Dryers

- Base mounting specifications
- Voltage, amperage, and phase requirements
- Gas supply requirements
- Venting requirements
- Air supply requirements
- Distance from combustible materials
- Maintenance access requirements
- Space requirements

PRACTICAL LIFE EXPECTANCY

The practical life expectancy of coin-operated washers can range from about 4 years to more than 15, depending on the make and the model. Dryers will generally outlast the washers. You need to know the practical life expectancy of the equipment before you make a purchase.

If you are inexperienced in the industry, talk with distributors, manufacturers, servicemen and other laundry owners. The information that you will gain will help you determine the practical life expectancy of the various brands and models of equipment you are considering.

COST-TO-REVENUE RATIO

Basically, this is the cost of the machine divided by the revenue it will produce. When comparing washers, <u>the lower the figure the better</u>. True cost includes freight and installation. It is also affected by practical life expectancy and the salvage value (trade-in value) of the machine at the end of its practical life. Since washer capacity varies among machines, revenue must be expressed as revenue per pound (dry weight) of washer capacity. Use the following formula to get the cost-to-revenue ratio:

$$\text{Cost-To-Revenue Ratio} = \left(\frac{\text{Installed Cost - Salvage Value}}{\text{Practical Life Expectancy}} \right) \div \left(\frac{\text{Revenue Per Cycle}}{\text{Dry Load Capacity}} \right)$$

If your washer costs $750 delivered and installed and you expect to get a $75 trade-in allowance at the end of 7 years (84 months), your cost factor is 8.035 ($750 - $75 ÷ 84). If the average weight of a full load of dry clothes is 8 pounds and the revenue per cycle is 75¢, the revenue per pound is .093¢ (.75 ÷ 8). When these figures are plugged into the formula, the cost-to-revenue ratio is 86:

$$\text{Cost-To-Revenue Ratio} = \left(\frac{\$750 - \$75}{84 \text{ Months}} \right) \div \left(\frac{75 \text{ Cents}}{8 \text{ Pounds}} \right) = \frac{8.035}{.093} = 86$$

Selecting Your Equipment

What is the cost-to-revenue ratio of a 20-pound capacity washer costing $1,710 installed with a 12-year practical life expectancy? If the estimated trade-in value is $400 and the revenue per cycle is $2.75, the cost-to-revenue ratio is 66. This is much better than the 8-pound capacity washer, but be sure to consider other factors, like energy efficiency and especially customer preference.

Remember, if your figures are inaccurate, your comparisons will be inaccurate. Working with formulas is like working with a computer. If you put garbage in, you will get garbage in return. (Make sure you read Chapters 6, 13 and 15 before making your cost-to-revenue comparisons.)

ENERGY EFFICIENCY

Since energy is a major expense, energy efficiency must be considered when you select the washers, dryers, and hot water heater. Some energy (electricity) is used to run the motors in washers and dryers. Most of the energy (natural gas or electricity) is used to heat water for the washers and to heat the dryer drums.

When you compare washers of equal capacity, compare the average hot water usage. When you compare dryers, compare the number of cubic feet of gas or the watts of electricity that are needed to evaporate a pound of moisture. The difference is insignificant between brands for the cost of electricity to run motors.

On the average, consumers select the hot wash 34 percent of the time, the warm wash 53 percent of the time, and the cold wash 13 percent of the time. Washer specification sheets should tell you the gallons of hot water per cycle that are used on hot wash and warm wash settings. If they don't, contact the manufacturer for this information.

A washer that uses 16 gallons of hot water on the hot wash setting, and 8 gallons of hot water on the warm wash setting will average 9.68 gallons of hot water per cycle. (This is 34 percent of 16, plus 53 percent of 8—or an average of 9.68 gallons.)

The extraction efficiency of your washers will affect the cost of drying the clothes in your dryers. A full load of wet clothes in

Coin Laundries — Road to Financial Independence

a 30-pound (dry clothes) capacity dryer could easily contain 26 pounds of water which must be evaporated. Removal of more water in the final spin reduces the amount of energy that is required to dry the clothes. Reducing the weight of a washed load of clothes by 1 pound can mean a 14-percent reduction in drying costs!

The water extraction efficiency of a washer is determined by spin speed, tub diameter, spin time, tub configuration, and whether the tub's spin axis is vertical or horizontal. It is usually expressed as the percentage of dry weight of a washed load of clothes. The lower the percentage, the better. In other words, an 8-pound washer with 190% water extraction efficiency will produce a washed load of clothes that weighs 15.2 pounds (1.9 • 8). This means that 7.2 pounds of water (15.2 - 8) must be removed by the dryer.

Water extraction figures are seldom found in washer specification sheets. You may have to contact the manufacturer to get this information. If you can't get this information, run your own tests! Find a coin laundry that has the brand of washer you are considering. Be sure that the machine is operating properly. Weigh a full load of clothes; then wash it and weigh them again. Divide the wet weight by the dry weight and you have your percentage of water extraction efficiency.

Trying to compare the energy efficiency of different brands of dryers by reading the specification sheets is like trying to sort fly specks from pepper. Few specification sheets give you the information necessary to make an accurate comparison. For example, the specification sheets for two brands of dryers might list the gas input as 80,000 B.t.u. per hour. In actual use, one dryer might take 20 percent longer to dry. This would make it to use more energy to get the same results.

Besides heat, drying efficiency depends on air flow, design of the dryer, and how the dryer is installed. The information you need for an accurate comparison is the number of B.t.u. of gas or watts of electricity that each dryer uses to evaporate a pound of moisture. You will probably have to write the manufacturers for this information. (More detailed information on the cost of operation of washers and dryers can be found in Chapter 15.)

As long as you are comparing energy efficiency, compare the total water usage of the washers you are considering. In some areas, water is very expensive. In other areas, sewer use (measured by your water consumption) is very expensive. Let's hope you're not faced with both situations.

CUSTOMER PREFERENCE

Carefully look at the comments on the Prospective Customer Data Sheets from your market survey. Your customers will go elsewhere to launder their clothes if they don't like your equipment. The type of customer you have often determines the type of equipment you will use. Blue-collar workers may wash big loads of work clothes in one large front-loading washer. White-collar workers, with their wide variety of clothes, may use several small washers operating at the same time on different program settings.

The same situation can influence which dryers you select. Blue-collar workers may like to dry all their clothes in one or two large, multiple-load dryers. White-collar workers may prefer to dry their clothes according to the way they were washed—in several smaller loads in stacked dryers. Here they can choose cycles according to the type of fabric they are drying.

Geography can also influence which laundry equipment you pick. If you have a coin laundry near a beach, you will need washers that are good at removing sand. After all, who wants to put their clothes into a washer that has an eighth-inch of sand in the tub? Sand also causes maintenance and cleaning problems for some machines.

DURABILITY

Your machines will be exposed to a great many people. Children climb on them, kick the cabinets, slam washer lids and swing on dryer doors like monkeys in a zoo. Sometimes adults aren't any better. Your equipment must be able to withstand this abuse, year after year.

If your laundry is unattended, you want your equipment to be as tamper-proof as possible. Washers and dryers with removable filters or other removable parts could be vulnerable to the theft of these items. Certain people will carry off anything that isn't screwed down—even when they have no use for it!

Abuse and vandalism are emotionally-charged problems, but don't be too concerned. Their cost in most locations is insignificant when compared to other operating costs and your potential profits. You can reduce vandalism and abuse by careful planning and good management.

SERVICE AND REPAIR

Anything that is mechanical will require service. The question is, "How much service?" Talk with other coin laundry owners to find out what problems they have with their equipment. Visit manufacturers and/or distributors of coin laundry equipment. While they may not tell you what problems they have with their equipment, they will be quick to point out the weaknesses of their competitors' machines. The independent machinery service companies in your area service a variety of brands and can tell you the strengths and weaknesses of the machines you are considering.

If you are considering top-loading washers, check *Consumers Reports* magazines at your local library. Consumers Union runs a survey on the frequency-of-repair for many brands of domestic top-loading washers. Since the mechanics of domestic and commercial washers are the same for most brands, much of the information about the domestic washers would apply to coin-operated ones.

Ask these questions when visiting manufacturers and distributors: How easy is it to maintain and service the equipment? Is service technical help available? Where? Is service training available to you? If so, at what cost? Find out where you are trained and how much time you will require for the course. You want to know how to maintain your equipment and what to do when it breaks down. A dead machine makes no money.

WARRANTY

Carefully compare the warranties of the equipment you are considering. A good warranty can save you a lot of money. Warranties are generally broken down into two sections: parts and labor. When comparing warranties, ask these questions:

- How long is the warranty?
- When does the warranty begin?
- What does the warranty cover?
- Who pays the labor?
- Who pays freight on the parts?
- What voids the warranty?
- Does the warranty specify the service firm?

Answers to these questions will quickly tell you which warranty is the best.

COST AND AVAILABILITY OF PARTS

No matter how good your equipment is, you will need parts from time-to-time. The washers and dryers, for example, will require motors, timers, pressure switches, pumps, control switches, belts, thermostats, gas valves, etc. Check the following for each brand of equipment you are considering:

- Parts cost
- Parts availability and source
- Parts order lead time
- Minimum order requirements
- Replacement parts warranty

Service on a machine can be a nightmare if parts aren't available or if they take weeks to arrive. You don't want a washer sitting idle for eight weeks while you wait for an expensive timer to be shipped from Europe. The shipping and handling costs alone could be out of sight.

Some parts may be stocked locally, but what about non-stock items? How soon can you get special items from the manufacturer or distributor? What do you do if it takes six weeks to get a part? Stock them yourself? Take a chance on losing money while your equipment sits idle? Time to reconsider your equipment selection.

Some companies require a minimum dollar amount on their parts orders. You either purchase a lot of unnecessary parts or end up paying $50 for a special bolt that normally sells for 50¢.

Are the replacement parts under warranty? What are the terms of the warranty? If a replacement part fails under warranty, who pays the freight on the returned part?—on the new part?

SAFETY

This is the age of consumer liability suits and skyrocketing liability insurance rates. Manufacturers of coin laundry equipment are acutely aware of this and take precautions to make sure that their products are safe. Injuries can occur, however, no matter how safe a product.

If you are involved in litigation, the court will probably determine that you have some share of the responsibility for an injury. Carefully examine the equipment you are considering and check the safety features before making a final buying decision.

MANUFACTURER AND DISTRIBUTOR ASSISTANCE

The quantity and quality of help you can expect from the equipment manufacturer and distributor is a factor when selecting equipment. Good equipment manufacturers or distributors can provide tremendous help. On the other hand, there is no end to the problems that can be caused by their sometimes inept or unscrupulous representatives.

Before purchasing your equipment, check the reputation of manufacturers and distributors with the Better Business Bureau. Talk with coin laundry owners who have had business dealings with them. Be very thorough. It could prevent trouble and save you considerable money later.

THE WATER HEATER

The water heater is the heart of your coin laundry. It will use more energy than any other single piece of equipment. Your laundry cannot run without it. Use the following criteria when comparing different brands of water heaters:

- Rated efficiency
- Life expectancy
- Installed cost
- Safety
- Warranty
- Availability of parts
- Availability of service technical help

Many self-service laundries are operating with oversized hot water heaters and oversized hot water storage tanks. This results in wasted energy and higher energy costs for the owners. An oversized heater will cycle on-and-off more often. The less a heater cycles (the longer that each cycle burns), the more efficient the heater.

Water heaters are measured by the amount of heat that they can produce. This heat is measured in British thermal units, or B.t.u. per hour. A B.t.u. is the amount of heat required to raise the temperature of one pound of water, one Fahrenheit degree. Gas companies sometimes use a larger unit of measurement called a "therm" which is 100,000 B.t.u. Your monthly gas usage on your gas bill is probably measured in therms.

Coin Laundries — Road to Financial Independence

Oversized water storage tanks waste energy. Storage tanks lose heat through the surface area. The larger the tank, the more heat lost. Therefore, more energy is required to maintain water temperature in the storage tank.

If oversized heaters and tanks are inefficient, why are so many coin laundries operating with oversized equipment? The main reason is that many coin laundry owners do not know how to determine the correct heater and tank size. They copy the heater and storage tank specifications from other coin laundries, which are wrong.

In other words, Fred is building a coin laundry and he decides to use a 1,000,000 B.t.u. heater because "ol' Joe over in West Spider's Breath, Montana has the same size laundry and that's what he uses. He never runs out of hot water." When ol' Joe built his laundry, washers used over 50 percent more hot water. Joe replaced the original washers with modern, energy efficient machines, but didn't resize his water heating system when it needed replacing. No wonder Joe never runs out of hot water. He could supply hot water for two coin laundries.

Here's how to figure out the correct heater and tank size. Obtain the following:

1. Maximum gallons of hot water used per cycle for each washer type
2. Maximum number of washer cycles per hour (including loading and unloading time) for each washer type
3. Lowest temperature of the supply water
4. Anticipated water heater setting
5. Water heater efficiency

The first two items can be determined from information on the washer specification sheets. Contact the water company for the temperature of the supply water in the winter months. You must decide on the temperature of the hot water. Generally, 120° water will be hot enough to satisfy the customers and much more economical to produce than temperatures of 145° or more.

92

Selecting Your Equipment

Information on the efficiency of the water heater should be on the specification sheet. If not, contact the manufacturer. Modern water heaters are generally around 75 percent efficient. That is, an input of 100,000 B.t.u. of gas would produce 75,000 B.t.u. of usable heat.

Since a B.t.u. is the amount of heat required to raise one pound of water one Fahrenheit degree, the maximum pounds per hour of hot water consumption times the number of degrees Fahrenheit that the water must be raised divided by the heater efficiency is the B.t.u. rating of the heater you will require. Water weighs 8.345 pounds per gallon, so the formula would be as follows:

$$\frac{\text{Washers} \cdot \text{Gallons} \cdot \text{Cycles} \cdot 8.345 \cdot \text{Temp. Rise}}{\text{Heater Efficiency}} = \text{B.t.u.}$$

Assume that you have a self-service laundry with 26 washers. Each of your washers uses a maximum of 16 gallons of hot water per cycle. Your washers can run 2 cycles per hour including loading and unloading time. The water company tells you that the lowest temperature of the supply water is 40°F. You want to maintain your hot water at 120°F. So your heater must raise the temperature 80°F.

If the water heater you are considering is 75 percent efficient, you will require a 740,590 B.t.u. heater:

$$\frac{26 \cdot 16 \cdot 2 \cdot 8.345 \cdot 80°}{.75} = 740,590 \text{ B.t.u.}$$

What if your coin laundry contains several different types of washers with varying hot water needs and cycle times? In this case, use the formula for each washer type and add the results together. The total will be the B.t.u. requirements of your heater.

The formula shows that a heater of approximately 750,000 B.t.u. will supply your hourly hot water needs. This assumes that the demand for hot water is evenly spread over the hour. It is not! A surge in demand will occur if all washers are set for maximum hot water usage and started at the same time.

93

Coin Laundries — Road to Financial Independence

Under these circumstances, your heater cannot produce hot water fast enough. Add a hot water storage tank to compensate for this uneven rate of demand. A hot water tank that will hold approximately 30 percent of the hourly hot water demand is generally considered sufficient to compensate for a surge in demand. Your laundry would require a 250-gallon hot water tank (26 • 16 • 2 • 30%).

It's unlikely that all washers in a self-service laundry would be set for maximum hot water use and started at the same time. The possibility of this occurring decreases as the number of washers increases. An adjustment can be made in the water heater size in coin laundries that have thirty or more washers. Reduce the heater size by 2 percent for every 5 additional washers over 25—up to 100 total washers as follows:

30 Washers	—	2 Percent Reduction
50 Washers	—	10 Percent Reduction
75 Washers	—	20 Percent Reduction
100 Washers	—	30 Percent Reduction

There has been a trend in recent years to use the <u>average</u> hot water usage of the washers rather than the <u>maximum</u> hot water usage when sizing the hot water heater. On the average, consumers select a hot wash 34 percent of the time and a warm wash 53 percent of the time. If your washers use 16 gallons of hot water on the hot wash setting and 8 gallons of hot water on the warm wash setting, the average hot water usage per cycle would be 9.68 gallons (34 percent of 16, plus 53 percent of 8).

Using 9.68 gallons in the formula instead of the maximum hot water usage of 16 gallons, the water heater size needed for the coin laundry in our previous example would be:

$$\frac{26 \cdot 9.68 \cdot 2 \cdot 8.345 \cdot 80°}{.75} = 448,058 \text{ B.t.u.}$$

Selecting Your Equipment

To help compensate for this lower rate of production, the size of your water tank should be increased substantially and thoroughly insulated to prevent heat loss.

If you are running a low-volume coin laundry and your business is spread fairly evenly throughout the week, you would probably have sufficient hot water to meet demand. A large storage tank would guarantee it. You would save on the cost of the water heating system and on energy costs. The smaller heater would operate more efficiently because it would cycle fewer times during hot water demand. A high-volume laundry, however, would likely run out of hot water several times on the weekends if the water heater was sized for average hot water use.

There are many brands and types of hot water heaters on the market. You will not be short of reading material when it comes time to study specification sheets. Categories of water heaters available for self-service laundries are:

- Heater and tank combination
- Heater and separate tank
- Multiple heaters and separate storage tank
- Tankless hot water heater

HEATER AND TANK COMBINATION

The heater and tank combination is similar to the type that is used in the home except that it is much larger. This type of heater is comparatively inexpensive and normally has a shorter life expectancy than the other types of heaters. Several heaters can be combined to get the required hot water output.

Other than initial cost, there are two main advantages of using this type of heater: it is easily installed and takes up less space. In some areas, municipal codes are not as strict with this type as with other types of heaters, particularly if several heaters of low B.t.u. output are used to meet hot water requirements.

HEATER AND SEPARATE TANK

The heater and separate storage tank is popular in medium to large laundries because it has a long life expectancy and is very efficient when properly installed. Space is needed for the hot water storage tank as well as for the heater. Installation cost is greater than for the heater-tank combination. While the initial cost of this heating system is higher than for the heater-tank combination, life expectancy must be considered when comparing costs.

MULTIPLE HEATERS AND SEPARATE STORAGE TANK

Multiple heaters can be used to balance the load requirements. This increases heater efficiency, which reduces energy costs. During slow periods, only one heater is needed to meet the demand for hot water. This is more efficient than a large heater that rapidly cycles on and off. During periods of peak hot water demand, the other heater (or heaters) provides backup.

This system has three disadvantages: a high equipment cost, high installation costs, and greater space requirements. Besides energy efficiency, a big advantage of this system is reliability. If one heater is shut down for maintenance or repair, the other can still supply hot water.

TANKLESS HOT WATER HEATERS

Tankless heaters are available in two types: the low pressure boiler and the instant hot water heater. Low pressure boilers derive some efficiency by heating the water at about 4 pounds pressure. Their design gives excellent heat transfer.

Instant hot water heaters are installed by placing several heaters in series. The heaters cycle on in stages, depending on the demand for hot water at the time. The laundry will not run out of hot water with either of these systems; however, the maximum rate of flow of hot water will depend on the thermostat setting and the temperature of the supply water.

Selecting Your Equipment

Tankless heaters take up very little space. Energy is consumed only when needed because the system is not required to maintain the temperature of hot water in a storage tank. The main disadvantage is that they will not meet the need for hot water during peak load times unless an unusually large boiler is used or an unusually large number of instant heaters are installed in series. It's not that you run out of hot water. The system just won't produce it fast enough to meet the demand.

These systems are generally sized for the average hot water requirement, which is measured in gallons of hot water per minute at a given temperature. Hot water flow slows down if the temperature of the supply water drops, such as during the cold winter months. If the demand for hot water exceeds the rate of production by the heating system, the cycle times of the washers are extended. You then lose revenue during peak load times.

Don't be discouraged by all the complex decisions you have to make when selecting equipment. Be encouraged! You now know more than most of the people who are now buying or building self-service laundries.

If a little knowledge is dangerous, where is the man who has so much as to be out of danger?

—Thomas Henry Huxley

11

PLANNING
YOUR LAYOUT

PLANNING YOUR STORE layout is no more difficult than arranging your furniture at home. It may even be easier because your coin laundry layout is planned on paper. Revisions are made with an eraser rather than by back-breaking lifting, pushing and shoving.

You don't need a technical background to plan a simple layout. Your experience finding the store location, surveying your market, planning the size of the store, and selecting the equipment prepared you. The layout is just an extension of your ideas based on these experiences.

Other than patience, imagination, and common sense, all you need are:

1. A pencil
2. A large eraser
3. A calculator (optional)

4. A ruler or straight edge
5. A pad of $1/4$-inch lined graph paper, approximately 16" by 22" in size

EQUIPMENT

Much of your work is already done. By now, you have the equipment specification sheets and the installation specifications for the equipment you selected. The specification sheets will give you the sizes of the equipment and the services you need: water, gas, electric, sewer and venting.

The equipment installation specification sheets provide:

- Floor anchoring diagrams
- Hookup specifications for the utilities
- Door swings
- Energy and water requirements
- Space requirements and access points for service and maintenance
- Venting and air supply specifications for the water heater and dryers

Most top-loading washers and stacked dryers will need 6-to 8-inches for utility service runs (water, gas, electric, sewer and venting) behind the machines when placed against a wall. If placed back-to-back, they will need 8-to 12-inches. Most front-loading washers and most large dryers require 2 feet of clearance in the back for service and maintenance.

Some manufacturers claim that an 18-inch clearance is sufficient. The trend has been to reduce the amount of space required behind the equipment for service and maintenance. Many manufacturers are locating access-panels in the front of the machines. Check the specification sheets carefully before making your layout. Here's why:

"It's busted, and it's gonna stay busted!" replied John, an inexperienced laundry owner, when a customer asked him about a large front-loader. John purchased the coin laundry and then built a cement block wall behind the washer. His mistake was obvious when the washer needed repair and a service technician was called. The machine couldn't be moved because it was bolted to a concrete pad by internal half-inch diameter bolts. The only access to the bolts was (You guessed it!) through the rear access-panel of the washer.

You can see how critical it is to read your specification sheets carefully.

AIR INTAKE AND EXHAUST VENTS

Clothes dryers and hot water heaters must be vented to the outside. Follow the venting instructions in the installation specification sheets. Pay attention to the length limitations for the vent pipe or your equipment will not operate properly.

As a rule, dryers will push air up to 30 feet through a straight pipe without losing much efficiency. Deduct 2 feet from the 30-foot maximum for each 45° turn, and 4 feet for each 90° turn. When venting great distances to a roof or outside wall, it's best to run the individual dryer vents into a large single duct that contains an inducer fan. Make sure you provide access-panels in the common duct on long horizontal runs. This makes it easy to clean out accumulated dirt and lint.

Gas clothes dryers and gas hot water heaters require air for combustion. Dryers also require air for circulation through the dryer drums. Twelve 30-pound-capacity dryers (operating at the same time) will move almost 10,000 cubic feet of air through the dryer drums and out the exhaust vents every minute. This would be all of the free air contained in a 1,000 square-foot store with a 10-foot-high ceiling!

Because of this, air (called "make-up air") must be supplied to this equipment from the outside. You do this by providing a screened opening(s) to the outside which is located near the equipment or by ducts from the outside to the equipment. You will need 1 square inch of free area for make-up air for every 1,000 B.t.u. of gas input.

If you are going to screen the openings against birds and animals, add an additional 10 percent.

Twelve gas dryers rated at 90,000 B.t.u. would require 1,080 square inches of opening for make-up air (90 sq. in. • 12 dryers). If you are going to screen the opening, add an additional 108 square inches (10%), for a total of 1,188 square inches. This is a 30-inch by 40-inch opening.

Some coin laundry owners use ducts for the intake-air and run the dryer vent pipe inside the intake-air ducts. This preheats the dryer intake-air and makes the dryer more energy efficient.

Be sure to allow enough space for duct work around your hot water heater when you plan the space requirements. For example, one installation specification sheet for a 1,000,000 B.t.u. hot water heater calls for two 22-inch by 25-inch air supply ducts. One is to enter the room over the heater and extend to approximately 6 inches below the ceiling line. The other is to be dropped to within 6 inches of the floor near the burner. Ducts of this size take up a lot of space.

All this sounds complicated, but it really isn't! The equipment installation specification sheets provides you with detailed information on venting and make-up air requirements for your equipment. Follow the instructions and you'll have no problem.

THE UTILITIES

Consider the routing of sewer pipe, water pipe, vent pipe, air intake ducts and electrical wiring when planning the laundry layout. The order of importance is:

1. Sewer lines
2. Venting and intake ducts
3. Water and gas lines
4. Electrical wiring

Since the sewer requires gravity, routing of the sewer line will have the most influence on your laundry layout. New construction gives you the greatest amount of design flexibility. You can install your sewer lines before the floor is poured.

If the concrete floor is already in place, sections must be cut with a diamond tipped concrete saw and removed. After the sewer lines are installed, the floor is patched with concrete and reinforcing mesh. This is time consuming and adds to your expense.

An alternative is to run the main sewer line along a wall. You can enclose the pipe with a false wall that is 36 inches high with a 6-inch to 8-inch ledge on top. The false wall can also house the water lines, gas lines and electrical wiring. These services can be extended into the space at a 90° angle to the false wall to serve groups of washers and/or dryers that are placed back-to-back. (See sample layout on pages 108 through 111.)

Venting and intake ducts normally enter and exit through the roof in single story buildings and through a side or rear wall in multi-story buildings. Horizontal ducts are hidden by a dropped ceiling. Water lines, gas lines, and electrical wiring are routed through walls or above the ceiling.

Some laundry owners run the water lines under the concrete floor with the sewer lines. This can save money on labor and materials, but look out pocketbook if they start to leak! Try and find it! What is worse, you could be paying for water that is seeping into the ground. Before buying one of these laundries, shut off all the equipment and watch the water meter. If it moves, you have a leak.

THE GENERAL LAYOUT

Since rent and rent-related costs are one of your largest expenses, plan to use as little space for your layout as is absolutely necessary to meet your objectives. Secondary aisles (aisles between washers) should be a minimum of 4 feet from any obstruction. Your main aisle(s) will have the greatest amount of foot traffic and should be a minimum of 6 feet in width.

Good planning can provide for a high-volume business in limited space. Concentrate on reducing the amount of cross traffic and total amount of foot travel. Typical coin laundry customers will enter the store several times with several loads of clothes. They usually stack the clothes on top of or in front of the washers that they intend to use. Here's the pattern of movement for a typical coin laundry customer:

- Automobile to washers
- Washers to coin or bill changer
- Changer to soap dispenser
- Soap dispenser to washers
- Washers to seating
- Seating to washers
- Washers to dryers
- Dryers to seating
- Seating to dryers
- Dryers to clothes-folding tables
- Clothes-folding tables to automobile

Plan your store to reduce the total number of steps that your customers must take when they use your laundry. This will mean more business volume with less confusion during peak load times. Your customers will be pleased.

You may want to consider a fenced play area for toddlers. This keeps them out of harms way and from bothering customers. It also reduces the amount of cleaning you must do. Everyone will be thankful.

Design your coin laundry so that it is spacious and well-lit. Customers feel more secure using a laundry that has plenty of window area, particularly if they can see everyone in the store before they enter. Eliminate hiding places or blind areas whenever possible. This will discourage vandalism and theft.

For added security, consider placing your coin and bill changers in a well-lit area near the front windows where they can always be observed from outside the building. Thieves won't like this.

Planning Your Layout

SEATING AND CLOTHES-FOLDING TABLES

Plan enough seating and clothes-folding tables to meet your customers' needs. A general rule-of-thumb is one seat for every two single-load washers. A 30-pound-capacity triple-load washer would count as three single-load washers.

The amount of clothes-folding table space you will need is another matter. This is influenced by:

* Layout
* Available space
* Projected load-spread
* Projected laundry volume
* Number of individual tables

Small laundries should have approximately 3 square feet of clothes-folding table space for every washer. Larger laundries may get by with as little as 2 square feet per washer if the business volume is expected to be spread evenly over the week. If you are going to be "packed" on the weekends, you had better figure on 3 square feet per washer.

Your customers will use as much clothes-folding table space as is conveniently within their reach. It's best to have several smaller clothes-folding tables rather than one large table that could be monopolized by a single customer.

CONSTRUCTION CODES

Building codes will influence your layout. For example, if you have a rest room, local code may specify the size and require it to be equipped for the handicapped. Codes may require you to use double-wall venting for vents that pass through combustible building materials. The swing direction, types of locks, and construction of doors are often determined by code requirements. You may have to use "exit" or other instructional signs and install a fire sprinkling system and/or fire extinguishers. Many fire codes specify that water heaters be located in a fire rated room at a specific distance from walls or combustible materials.

Building and fire codes vary considerably throughout the country, so check with local inspectors during planning to discuss layout ideas and seek advice. Most building and fire inspectors are helpful. You'll save a lot of time and effort on revisions if you contact these inspectors early in the planning stage.

DECORATING

Give careful consideration to your ceiling, floor, walls and fixtures, particularly if your laundry is unattended. Customers and their children are unsupervised in unattended coin laundries, so select building materials and fixtures that are resistant to hard use.

A good example is floor covering. Carpeted floors are comfortable and attractive, and they reduce noise level. Laundry customers like carpet, but carpet is easily damaged by chemical spills, cigarette burns, and other hazards. It also requires frequent cleaning.

Ceramic tile is very durable and easy to maintain, but the initial material and installation expense is very high. Tile is susceptible to chipping and it does nothing to reduce noise. Most ceramic tile is very slippery when wet, especially if water comes in contact with soap spills.

Composition tile does little to reduce noise. On the other hand, some brands are highly durable, easy to maintain, and resist burns and chemical spills. If you use composition tile, pick a pattern that doesn't get slippery when wet.

HELP WITH YOUR LAYOUT

Don't worry about laying out your coin laundry. You will not run short of ideas! Visit other coin laundries and look at their design. You can also get firsthand proof of how durable various

Planning Your Layout

building materials are. Coin laundry equipment manufacturers and distributors have an endless supply of pictures, brochures and layout ideas to draw upon, too.

Some equipment distributors will even supply a layout kit that contains a large plastic layout sheet with lines resembling graph paper. You outline your store floor with grease pencil. Next you make trial arrangements on the layout sheet with miniature scale models of washers, dryers and clothes-folding tables.

Some equipment distributors will even draft store layouts for you as an added service. These layouts can be quite helpful, but they should not substitute for your own good judgment. After all, you will profit from your business, but you will pay for any mistakes—no matter who makes them! A good investment is to have a coin laundry consultant analyze your layout and recommend revisions. Do this before you start construction.

There is usually more than one way to lay out a coin laundry in a given space. It's not unusual to develop five or more hand-drawn layouts on quarter-inch lined graph paper before you select the final one. From this you will draw (or have someone draw) an equipment layout blueprint. A layout as it was made on graph paper and the resulting equipment layout blueprint is shown on pages 108 through 111.

Submit the equipment layout blueprint along with copies of the machinery specifications and installation sheets to carpenters and to plumbing, sheet metal, and electrical contractors for preliminary cost estimates. Be sure to do this prior to signing your lease.

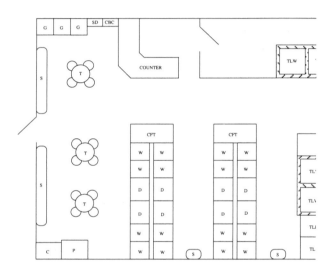

COIN LAUNDRY

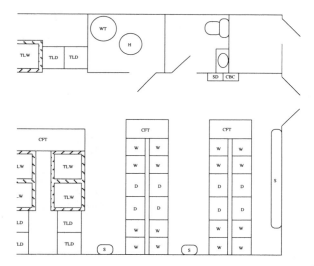

G	–	Game
T	–	Table
S	–	Seating
P	–	Pop Machine
H	–	Water Heater
C	–	Candy Machine
D	–	Stacked Dryers
W	–	Top Load Washer
WT	–	Water Tank
SD	–	Soap Dispenser
TLD	–	Triple Load Dryer
CBC	–	Coin/Bill Changer
TLW	–	Triple Load Washer
CFT	–	Clothes Folding Table

LAYOUT SKETCH

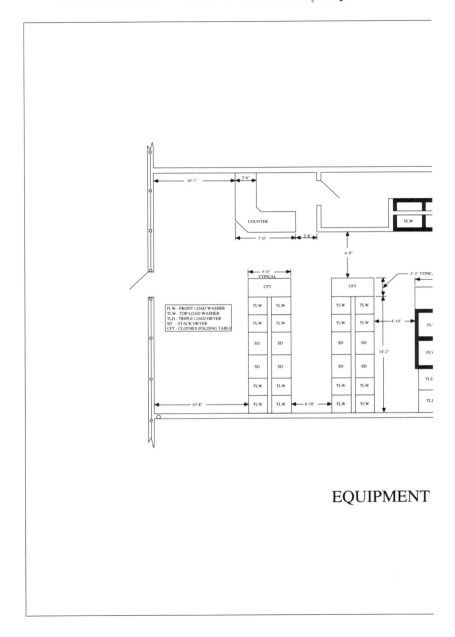

EQUIPMENT

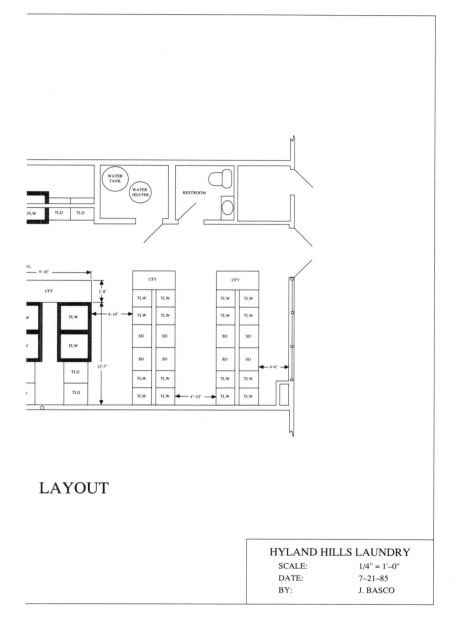

LAYOUT

HYLAND HILLS LAUNDRY	
SCALE:	1/4" = 1'–0"
DATE:	7–21–85
BY:	J. BASCO

Coin Laundries — Road to Financial Independence

> It is common sense to take a method and try it. If it fails, admit it frankly and try another. But above all, try something.
>
> —Franklin Delano Roosevelt

12

NEGOTIATING THE BEST LEASE POSSIBLE

YOUR LEASE IS the most important contract that you will sign. Rent is one of your biggest monthly operating expenses and you are in debt to your landlord the instant that both of you sign. You must make rent payments to the landlord whether your business succeeds or fails, unless a bankruptcy court judge waives this by decree.

It's important to have a good lease. It defines your rights. This means that a landlord cannot impose arbitrary rules on your business. It protects your investment. Consider the large amount of money you will spend for the leasehold improvements and equipment. In addition, the lease can add to (or detract from) the value of your laundry if you decide to sell it. *Never sign a lease unless it is thoroughly examined by a competent attorney.*

Most entrepreneurs are long on action and short on patience. Yet patience is the negotiator's most important tool. To be a successful negotiator, you must:

- Be patient
- Understand the other person's position
- Know how to develop and analyze proposals
- Be able to communicate well

If you lose patience, no amount of insight, planning ability, or skillful communication can save you from getting the short end of the deal.

Many landlords know little about the modern self-service laundry. They carry mental images of the rundown, dirty coin laundries of the past. You must overcome this image before you can expect to negotiate a favorable lease. Many landlords have even refused to lease space for coin laundries when the image problem was not handled.

Your first step in the lease negotiation is to sell the landlord. It's easier to get what you want from landlords who want your business in their shopping centers. A successful selling job means:

- Faster and easier negotiation
- A more favorable lease
- Fewer expenses

Shopping center owners consider three things when adding a new business to their center:

1. Is the business compatible with the other businesses in the shopping center?
2. Will the business bring new customers to the center?
3. Is the business likely to succeed?

Expect to be interviewed by the landlord, who will try to determine if you are financially responsible and if you have sufficient knowledge, experience, and skills to succeed.

Your landlord wants to get as much rent as possible. Shopping center owners do this by assembling the best combination of businesses to generate as much retail volume as possible. If you can convince the landlord that your business will help to do this, you will be negotiating from a position of strength.

Begin your negotiations with a written proposal. List your reasons for selecting the location. Provide the results of your market survey. Include a copy of your coin laundry layout. Use the following format for your written proposal:

1. **Sell the concept.** Provide a written description of your coin laundry. Include a copy of the proposed laundry layout. Provide brochures on the equipment you have selected for your laundry. Obtain pictures of similar self-service coin laundries from equipment manufacturers and distributors, and submit these with your proposal. If pictures are not available, locate some modern self-service laundries and photograph them yourself.

2. **Show why the coin laundry will be successful.** You gathered a tremendous amount of valuable information when you selected your location and did your market survey. This information convinced <u>you</u> that your business would be successful. Now write it up and use it to convince your landlord.

3. **Explain what your coin laundry will do for the landlord.** The Prospective Customer Data Sheets from your market survey will show that many of your prospects are buying their groceries and doing their shopping in other shopping centers. Your promotions will be directed toward those prospective customers, substantially increasing customers for other stores in the center. The landlord will collect more rent from these other stores based on the increase in their sales volume.

4. **State your personal qualifications.** This proposal is a good start. It will probably be the best that the landlord has seen, if not the <u>only</u> one. Your ability and general experi-

115

ence, combined with the information in this book, will make you better qualified to start this business than many experienced entrepreneurs. At the very least, you'll know more than any beginning entrepreneur. Include a copy of your financial statement in this section of your proposal.

5. **Include a revised copy of the landlord's lease.** Make sure to have your attorney review the lease <u>before</u> you present it to the landlord.

The lease will contain many items that need to be negotiated. One thing common to all leases is that they are written to protect the landlord, not the tenant. It's up to you to initiate revisions that are in your best interests. Now let's look at some points common to most leases:

BASIC RENT

Basic rent, normally paid monthly, is the amount of money that is charged for the store space. It is a fixed expense, not affected by variations in the volume of business.

Basic rent is highly negotiable, particularly if the landlord understands the positive impact that your laundry will have on the shopping center. Obviously, you want to keep your rent as low as possible. Find out the monthly rent that is being charged per square foot for similar retail space in similar shopping centers. If it's to your advantage, use this information in your negotiations.

PERCENTAGE RENT

Some leases specify that when the gross volume of a business reaches a certain level, the landlord receives a percentage of the gross volume. This can be in addition to the basic rent or as a replacement. In either case, you pay higher rent for the store space if the gross sales volume exceeds that certain level.

Negotiating the Best Lease Possible

For example, a lease might specify basic rent of $10.00 per square foot per year for a 2,000 square-foot space. It might have a provision that the tenant pays the monthly basic rent or 6 percent of the total sales receipts, whichever is greater. In this example, monthly basic rent would be $1,666.67. This would not increase unless gross sales exceeded $27,777.83 for the month, highly unlikely for a self-service coin laundry.

Coin laundries are generally considered low gross volume businesses. They have a high profit-to-revenue ratio. Percentage rent will not apply in most cases, but carefully analyze this clause to make sure that it will not have an adverse affect on your business.

ESCALATION CLAUSE

Because of high annual inflation rates in recent years, landlords have become wary of signing long-term leases at fixed rental rates. This has resulted in wide use of the escalation clause, which raises the basic rent at predetermined times during the life of the lease. The most common methods for determining basic rent escalation are:

- Fixed Rate
- Consumer Price Index (C P.I.)
- Percent of C.P.I.

The fixed rate of increase means that the basic rent will be increased by a specified dollar amount (or percentage) on specific dates. The advantage of this formula is that you know what future rental payments will be and can plan for them. The disadvantage is that you are locked into higher future rent payments even if the economy is sluggish, flat, or in decline.

The consumer price index is the monthly economic barometer used by the Federal government. It signals changes in the cost of living by measuring price increases (or decreases) in selected

117

consumer products or services such as housing, food, clothing, automobiles, or utilities.

Many leases periodically adjust basic rent according to the C.P.I. If the C.P.I. shows a cost of living increase of 4 percent, the basic rent is increased by 4 percent. The disadvantage is that you never know what the rent will be from year to year.

In recent years we have had double-digit inflation. Energy costs increased dramatically. The result was that many coin laundry owners suffered rent and utility increases at the same time. This plays havoc with your profits. Basic rent that is raised by a percentage of the C.P.I. is much easier on you. It is the lesser of the three evils, provided the percentage is not too high.

There are many variations on the above. Landlords and their attorneys can get quite imaginative when drawing up escalation clauses. Give careful consideration to any escalation clause before signing the lease. If possible, try to eliminate it.

COMMON AREA EXPENSES

Many leases require you to pay a portion of the expense of operating and maintaining the shopping center. This is usually prorated to you on the basis of how much of the total amount of leasable merchandising area in the shopping center you occupy. In other words, if the shopping center has 40,000 square feet of leasable store space and you lease 2,000 square feet, you pay $2,000/40,000$ths or 5 percent of the common area operating and maintenance charges.

The following monthly charges are examples taken from an actual lease:

    Management fee
    Utility room charge
    Water, sewer and trash removal
    Shopping center sign rental
    Parking lot lights

Landscaping and parking lot maintenance
Security service
Sprinkler equipment maintenance
Real estate and personal property taxes
Public liability and property damage insurance
Building maintenance

Some landlords overcharge tenants for these expenses because they have no incentive to keep them in line. Take every precaution against this. Even if your landlord has a reputation for being honest, there is no guarantee that the shopping center won't be sold to someone who is dishonest.

Determine the basis for each expense. Next, place a limit or "cap" on each expense. Make sure that the total of all common area expenses does not exceed a fixed percentage of your basic rent. Have your attorney amend the lease to protect you from excess common area charges. You have enough expenses of your own without paying an unfair share of your landlord's.

RIGHT TO AUDIT

Many leases give the landlord the right to audit your books, particularly if there is a percentage rent clause in the lease. Negotiate your right to audit the landlord's books, especially those operating and maintenance expenses that will be billed to you.

LENGTH OF LEASE AND RENEWAL OPTION

With the high cost of equipment and leasehold improvements, it's unwise to consider a short-term lease. Most laundry owners expect to be in a location for a minimum of ten to twelve years, and some for twenty years. The majority of coin laundry leases are for a ten to twelve-year period with an option to renew the lease for an additional five to six years.

Some laundry owners prefer a five-year lease with 2 five-year options. The advantage of the shorter base term is that you can discontinue the lease at the end of five years if the location proves unsatisfactory. The main disadvantage is that the rent could substantially increase if you elect to renew the lease.

RENEWAL OPTION

Unless you make a provision for arriving at a reasonable rent, you will be at the mercy of the landlord when it comes time to act on the option. You may have an option to renew the lease, but there is nothing to prevent the landlord from increasing the rent 1,000 percent to get rid of you.

Try to negotiate a fixed basic rent or at least a maximum percentage of increase in basic rent. If you cannot do this, then the basis for establishing the rent should be specified in the lease. The following example is taken from an actual lease:

SECTION 1.05. If tenant desires to renew the lease upon the premises herein described, tenant shall, on or before sixty (60) days prior to expiration of the original term, notify landlord in writing, by certified mail, of his intent to request the renewal of a lease upon the said premises, and shall state the amount of rental tenant is desirous of paying for the said premises for an additional period of five (5) years, and if landlord is in accord with the proposal thus made, the proposal shall be accepted in writing by landlord and sent to tenant by certified mail within five (5) days after receipt of the request of renewal. If landlord refuses to accept the proposal made by tenant, he shall so notify tenant and if landlord and tenant cannot agree upon the terms of an extension, then each of the parties hereto shall select an arbitrator to determine the amount of rental, and if the two arbitrators cannot agree, then the two arbitrators shall select a third arbitrator and the findings of two of the three arbitrators thus selected shall be final and binding upon both parties hereto. If the two arbitrators selected are unable to agree upon a third arbitrator, then a request shall be made of the Presiding Judge of the Circuit Court of the State of Oregon for the County of Washington to select such third arbitrator.

COMMENCEMENT OF LEASE TERM

There is no income while the coin laundry is under construction. You will save a lot of money if you negotiate a rent-free construction period in the lease. At 85¢ per square foot per month, savings in basic rent for a 90-day construction period would be $5,100 for 2,000 square feet of space. Savings would be even more if common area expenses were deferred during the construction period.

USE OF PREMISES

Your lease will specify the business (or type of business activity) that you can conduct in (or from) the leased space. Give this careful consideration. Businesses can change in 10 to 12 years, and you may want to add other services or even other businesses. The landlord can prevent you from doing this unless these services or businesses are listed in the lease. It's also important to have the exclusive right to conduct these businesses in the shopping center.

FEES OR DUES FOR SHOPPING CENTER ADVERTISING OR MERCHANTS ASSOCIATION

Many leases require you to join and pay dues to an association of merchants in the shopping center. They may also require you to contribute advertising funds for promoting the shopping center. If you cannot negotiate this out of the lease, at least put a lid on this expense, such as, "the total of these expenses are not to exceed three-quarters of one percent (.75%) of the gross sales for the month."

SIDEWALK, STREET AND WINDOW ADVERTISING

Leases often prohibit (or limit) the use of signs on the store-front and in the store windows. They can also restrict (or prohibit) the use of temporary or mobile signs on the sidewalk or in the parking lot. Few people realize how much influence these signs and displays have on the success of a retail business. Be sure that there are no restrictions in the lease that would prevent you from promoting your self-service laundry and its services. If you over-look these restrictions now, you'll be sorry later.

USE OF COMMON AREAS

"Common areas" means everything that is outside the leased premises but inside the boundaries of the shopping center. They include the parking lot, sidewalks, lights, signs, and landscaping. They also include the building exterior walls and roof.

Study all provisions of this section of the lease very carefully. The success of your laundry is totally dependent on convenient and adequate parking. If adequate and convenient parking is not guaranteed by the lease, look elsewhere for store space.

There have been cases in which a lease allowed the landlord to "redesignate the merchandising area." As a result, restaurants and other businesses were built in the parking lot. This severely reduced the number of parking spaces and obscured the fronts and entries of many of the retail stores.

When you review the lease, pay close attention to:

- Parking
- Lighting
- Signs
- Trash Removal and Cleaning

Have a sufficient number of convenient parking spaces designated for your laundry. Have the spaces painted or erect a sign at the head of each space. Coin laundries are generally open when dark, particularly in the winter. If the laundry parking areas and storefront aren't adequately lit, your customers may go elsewhere.

Be sure that your signs and displays are not blocked by landscaping or other obstructions. They should be seen from the main roads. Your lease should provide for <u>adequate</u> trash removal and <u>adequate</u> common area cleaning. You don't need a mess in front of your laundry every Friday and Saturday night.

MAINTENANCE OF BUILDING AND COMMON AREAS

Avoid conflict between you and your landlord by clearly defining who is responsible for what.

UTILITIES AND MUNICIPAL SERVICES

Utilities and services include:

- Sewer
- Water
- Gas
- Electric

Most landlords provide these services to the leased space. In your case, the volume or size of these services may not be adequate, and they may not meet code requirements. Make every effort to have the landlord provide these services to your specifications. If you succeed, you will save thousands of dollars in construction costs.

As mentioned in Chapter 9, sewer and water hookup fees can be sizeable. You can save thousands of dollars by negotiating with your landlord. The fees that were paid by the shopping center owner at the time of construction may be sufficient to satisfy part (if not all) of the fees that may be imposed on you by local government.

Coin Laundries — Road to Financial Independence

It's not unusual to discover that neither your landlord nor the government knows whether or not these requirements have been met. Answers to these questions are often arbitrary. Great patience is required to wade through the regulatory maze of the bureaucracy, but it will be time well spent if you save thousands of dollars. What you need to find out is:

- What fees have been paid by the shopping center?
- How were they determined?
- To what extent is the center using the services for which the fees were paid?
- Can the surplus amount be applied to your coin laundry?

There may be other opportunities to save money. Try using the shopping center's water (if the supply is adequate) and an in-line meter. This can save the high cost of having the water company tap into the main line and install their water meter.

Your landlord should provide adequate gas and electricity to your space. Specify this in the lease. Make sure that the lease also specifies the electrical amperage, voltage and phase that you need. Natural gas should be available in the quantities and pressures that are needed.

Modify the lease to protect yourself from any unforeseen utility hookup charges or fees. The following was taken from an addendum to a lease that was negotiated by a coin laundry owner:

"The landlord agrees to pay and be solely responsible for any other utility service hookup fees, start up costs or other charges that are or may be required by governmental entity or provider of utility services prior to or concurrent with the start of any utility service to the leased premises."

LEASEHOLD IMPROVEMENTS

Improvements can be ceilings, floors, walls, doors, windows, plumbing, electrical, heating, and air conditioning, but are not necessarily limited to these items. Some leases specify improvements that a landlord is willing to make (and pay for) to the leased premises. Other leases offer you allowances for making your own improvements. This area is wide open for creative negotiation. You can substantially reduce your construction costs here.

Get the specifications for each improvement offered by the landlord, and set a dollar value for each. Next, establish the option of taking cash for the improvement or applying the cash value to another leasehold improvement. For example, you might trade carpet for a ceiling with lights.

Sometimes you can save money by doing the contracting for the improvement rather than relying on the landlord. You can get more "bang for the buck" if you do the work yourself.

All agreements should be put in writing and added to the lease, either as a main section in the lease or by addendum. An example of a lease addendum used by one multi-store owner is presented on pages 127 and 128.

LEASE ASSIGNMENT AND SUBLETTING

You must maintain the right to assign the lease or to sublet the space to another party. Many leases provide these rights to you, subject to the consent of the landlord. If this right is based on the landlord's consent, the lease should specify that "consent shall not be unreasonably withheld."

Someday you may want to sell your business. If the going rent for similar space is higher than your rent, you can make additional money by subletting the space rather than assigning the lease. You charge higher rent to the new owner and pay the landlord the rent specified in the lease. The difference is yours to keep.

SETTLEMENT OF DISPUTES

What about a dispute with your landlord? This is a common occurrence, and settling these differences can get quite expensive, particularly when attorneys are involved. Establish your right to recover attorney fees and all costs incidental to enforcing the provisions of the lease, whether or not suit is brought, if you establish that your landlord is in default.

By now you can see the value of patience in lease negotiations. You will attend many meetings before a satisfactory lease emerges. Eliminate confusion by confirming all agreements in writing immediately after each meeting. You may be negotiating only one lease. The landlord may be negotiating ten and may not remember what was agreed upon fifteen minutes after your meeting.

Good negotiators win points by subtle and skillful use of leverage. Make the landlord want your coin-operated laundry in the shopping center. Make sure that the landlord is aware that you are negotiating with other shopping centers in the area. This puts you in a position of strength.

Of course, the lease agreement should be subject to your ability to get adequate financing. And it's worth repeating: ***Don't consider signing the lease without the advice of a competent attorney.***

Negotiating the Best Lease Possible

LEASE ADDENDUM

Lessor shall install or the demised premise will contain the following items:

1. Install glass storefront together with pair 36" double acting indexing door (or one 42" double acting indexing door) and 42" rear door, both to be located as shown in Lessee's plan. Front and back to be keyed alike with cylinder locks both sides.

2. Floor—Kentile (or equal) vinyl floor tile with wall base or DuPont Antron III (or equal) commercial nylon carpet with wall base, or a combination of both carpet and tile. Color is to be our selection.

3. Walls—High grade flat enamel paint. Color to be selected by Lessee and approved by Landlord. Walls to be finished and suitable for paneling or wallpaper.

4. Ceiling—Material to be approved by Lessee. Ceiling is to be a uniform 10-foot height throughout.

5. Rest room facilities per code but not less than one (1) water closet, one (1) wash basin, mirror, towel dispenser, and toilet tissue dispenser. Room to be located per Lessee's plans.

6. Air Conditioning—Provide and install two (2) evaporative cooling units having a minimum capacity of 8,500 c.f.m. each, or larger depending on the size of the building. Each unit to be controlled by thermostats enclosed in lock boxes.

7. Electrical—Provide electrical switches and porcelain receptacles in the rest room, equipment area, and back of dryers, and provide a 5-foot flex conduit pigtail for a dollar bill changer per Lessee's plan. Install 4-light Slimline fluorescent fixtures and tubes per Lessee's plan. Provide and install outside sign outlets to be controlled by time clock.

8. Install 2" water meter and extend 2" water line, or larger if required by code, to the inside wall of equipment room with shutoff valve.

9. Install a 2" gas line, or larger if required by code, to the inside wall of the equipment room with shutoff valve.

10. Install a 6" i.d. sewer line to the inside wall of equipment room in accordance with Lessee's plan.

11. Install 600 ampere power service (or larger if required by code), three-phase, 60 cycle, 220 volt, and power-panels with required amount of breakers per Lessee's plans. Meter to be outside building.

12. Cement floor including pads and recesses per Lessee's plans.

13. Provide and install all dryer and heater vents from finished ceiling through roof with roof-flashings and candy-canes per Lessee's plans and local code. Provide and install all gravity and combustion-air vents from finished ceiling through roof with roof-flashings and caps per Lessee's plan and local code.

14. Provide adequate heating.

ACCEPTED AND APPROVED:

By_____ Date_____

By_____ Date_____
                  (Lessor)

ACCEPTED AND APPROVED:

By_____ Date_____

By_____ Date_____
                  (Lessee)

13

ESTIMATING EQUIPMENT COSTS

E QUIPMENT AND RELATED expenses will represent 60 to 80 percent of the total cost of building your new self-service laundry. When estimating the cost of your equipment, look at the following costs:

- Freight charges
- Equipment loading, unloading and handling charges
- Equipment storage charges
- Materials-handling equipment rental
- Installation parts and installation tool rental
- Labor charges for installation

These expenses can be 10 to 20 percent of the cost of your equipment. Don't be shocked when the bills arrive.

FREIGHT CHARGES

The terms of shipment will be on price quotations and sales orders. Shipping terms are legal terms. You need to understand what they mean and how they can affect you. Just because you didn't understand the shipping terms doesn't mean that you can break the contract. Ignorance of the law is no excuse.

The term "f.o.b." means "free on board." When you see "f.o.b. truck," or "f.o.b. factory (or warehouse)" after a price, it means that it includes free delivery from the factory or warehouse to (and loaded into) the carrier at the point of departure. You pay all further transportation costs.

Under most shipping terms, you are responsible for making a claim and collecting the money for any loss or damage to the equipment after it is loaded on the carrier. In other words, if the truck is in a wreck, you have no recourse against the seller. You will have to file a claim with the carrier for damages.

Some manufacturers will assist you in collecting claims from the carrier, but only as a service. They are not legally obligated to do so. Be sure to contact your insurance agent and arrange for full business insurance coverage prior to starting construction or ordering equipment.

The following are five of the most common shipping terms:

1. f.o.b. (carrier and/or point of departure)

Sometimes written "f.o.b. (carrier and/or point of departure), freight collect." Under this term, you are quoted a price for equipment only. It is up to you to determine what the freight charges will be. Upon delivery, you pay the freight to the delivering carrier, usually by certified check. The seller assumes no responsibility for the equipment after it is loaded on the carrier. This is the most common method of shipment in the industry.

2. f.o.b. (carrier and/or point of departure), freight prepaid to (named destination)

The seller quotes either a delivered price or a price for the equipment only. The seller pays the freight to the carrier and then

130

invoices you for the the equipment and freight. The seller assumes no responsibility for the equipment after it is loaded on the carrier at the point of departure.

3. f.o.b. (carrier and/or point of departure), freight allowed to (named destination)

The seller quotes a delivered price. You pay the freight to the delivering carrier when the shipment arrives. The seller deducts the cost of the freight from your invoice. The seller assumes no responsibility for the equipment after it is loaded on the carrier at the point of departure.

4. f.o.b. (carrier and/or point of departure), freight allowed and prepaid to (named destination)

The seller quotes a delivered price. The seller pays the freight to the carrier. Again, the seller does not assume any responsibility for the equipment after it is loaded on the carrier at the point of departure.

5. f.o.b. (named destination)

The seller quotes a delivered price. The seller pays the freight and assumes all responsibility for the equipment until it is delivered to the named destination.

In 1–4, you assume full responsibility for filing loss or damage claims. If there is loss or damage during transit, you must file a claim with the delivering carrier. If you see massive damage when the shipment arrives, it may be best to reject the entire load. *Don't sign anything until you are sure that the merchandise is in good condition.* Make sure your insurance will cover loss or damage before ordering your equipment.

When reviewing the shipping terms on equipment quotations, make sure you have answers to the following questions:

1. Is the price a delivered price, or is it only for the equipment?
2. How much is the freight?

3. Who pays the freight to the carrier?
4. If you pay the freight: Do you pay the freight to the seller or the carrier? If the carrier—will you be invoiced, or do you pay the driver? Do you pay by bank check, certified check, or personal check?
5. When does the seller's responsibility for loss or damage end?

Since deregulation started in 1980, freight companies have become highly competitive in their rates and routes. Check freight rates with several carriers who normally haul from the point of departure to your destination. Don't get bogged down in details and technicalities. Get a total freight charge, in writing if possible, on the entire shipment. Do this by supplying the following information to the freight line:

1. Point of departure
2. Destination
3. Size, weight and contents of each carton

Example: 24 cartons washers each $47^1/_8$" high, $27^5/_8$" wide, $29^5/_8$" deep weighing 238 pounds per carton, and 12 cartons dryers each 76" high, $36^1/_4$" wide, $30^1/_2$" deep weighing 366 pounds per carton

Don't rely on "estimated" freight charges in quotations. Always check their accuracy with the carrier, even when they are quoted as being factual rather than estimated. Carefully audit all freight bills to make sure you have not been overcharged, particularly when the truck has been routed to two or more destinations. It's not uncommon to find that some freight recipients are overcharged and others undercharged. Abuses are common.

Upon delivery, examine all cartons carefully before signing the freight bill. Any dented, crushed or "suspect" cartons should be opened immediately and the contents examined in the presence of the driver. Note any damaged or missing items on the freight bill and have the driver sign it. The carrier will deny your claim if you don't follow this procedure.

If damaged merchandise is discovered later in a perfectly sound carton, stop unpacking immediately and call the delivering carrier for an immediate inspection. Save the carton and the packing material. Damage of this type is commonly known as "hidden damage." Hidden damage claims are difficult (although not impossible) to collect from the freight line.

EQUIPMENT LOADING, UNLOADING AND HANDLING CHARGES

These are mainly labor charges and include the cost of unloading the shipments when they arrive. They may also include labor charges for loading the machinery and equipment into and out of temporary storage facilities. Distributors have been known to charge "handling charges" on the invoice for the rental of equipment they used in their own warehouse to load the order.

EQUIPMENT STORAGE CHARGES

Equipment shipments cannot always be coordinated to arrive exactly when needed. Temporary storage space must often be located and rented when shipments arrive early. It's not a bad idea to locate adequate storage facilities before you order your equipment. More than one irate truck driver has stood around while a frantic laundry owner tried to figure out where to put an early arriving truckload of equipment.

MATERIALS-HANDLING EQUIPMENT RENTAL

This includes the cost of purchasing or renting equipment that you will use to load, unload, transport, or position the machines. You may need a fork lift, an appliance moving dolly, an unloading ramp, and possibly a pallet jack for moving heavy machinery. You may need to rent a portable hoist to lift evaporative coolers or air conditioners onto the roof. Chain or cable hoists can be rented and used for positioning equipment or for handling other heavy items. Rolling large machines around on pieces of 4-inch diameter pipe can often save on materials-handling equipment rental.

INSTALLATION PARTS AND INSTALLATION TOOL RENTAL

Special parts or tools that you require for installing the machines fall into this category. The following are examples:

Duct tape
Cement drill rental
Washer base grout
Vent pipe and screws
Foundation anchor bolts
Gas dryer flex couplings
Hoses and hose adaptors
Electrical appliance cords
Mounting bolts and screws
Anchor bolt placement templates

LABOR CHARGES FOR INSTALLATION

This includes the cost of hiring someone to help you install your equipment. Most laundry owners do the installation themselves with the help of family or friends.

Make a detailed list of everything you need for your self-service laundry. The following can be used as a guideline:

Equipment

• Washers
• Dryers

• Hot water heater and tank
• Soap dispenser

Estimating Equipment Costs

- Coin/bill changer
- Coin counter
- Unit heater
- Security system*
- Clothes-folding tables
- Seating
- Evaporative cooler

Equipment Related Expenses

- Freight charges
- Equipment loading, unloading and handling charges
- Equipment storage charges
- Materials-handling equipment rental
- Installation parts and installation tool rental
- Labor charges for installation

Miscellaneous

- Trash containers
- Clock
- Exterior signs**
- Etc.

   * Many local governments require a permit to install a security system.

** Exterior sign specifications must be approved by the landlord and the local municipality.

Get firm written bids from manufacturers or distributors for the equipment on your list. Be accurate and detailed in describing the equipment. Don't make the bidder guess what you want.

Make sure that the equipment in the quotation is complete and ready to install. You don't want to learn after the washers arrive that the locks, keys and coin slides were not in the bid. If you have to purchase these separately, they can cost you 10 percent of what you paid for the washer, and this doesn't include shipping charges.

Most quotations are written on the manufacturer's or distributor's form. No matter what it's called, it becomes a legally binding contract when signed by both parties. These contracts are written by the seller's attorneys. They protect the seller—not you.

Coin Laundries — Road to Financial Independence

Carefully read the contract when you are alone and not under pressure from the seller. The wording on many of these contracts will terrify you. Let your attorney read the important contracts before you sign. At the very least, rewrite what you don't like and make the seller acknowledge this by signing.

All sales contracts call for a down payment. Most specify that the seller keeps the down payment if the buyer cancels the agreement. Don't accept this if the seller isn't required to make shipment at a _specific_ price, on _specific_ items, within a _specific_ time frame.

One laundry owner received partial delivery of his equipment six months late. While waiting for it to arrive, he paid $12,000 rent on store space that produced no income. Make sure you have a "penalty clause" that makes sellers financially responsible for your losses if they fail to perform according to the terms of the contract.

Equipment pricing is flexible. A 40-percent markup on cost is not unusual. Some equipment is marked up as high as 60 percent. You can save a lot of money if you negotiate the following areas that are generally flexible:

- Equipment price
- Partial or full payment of freight by seller
- Extended parts and/or labor warranty by seller
- Installation of the equipment by the seller
- Installation assistance from seller
- Loan of installation tools and equipment by seller
- Seller to furnish parts and materials required for installation
- Free use of seller's warehouse for temporary storage
- Assistance by seller in unloading or moving the equipment
- Loan of materials-handling equipment by seller

While you can save money by skillful negotiations, remember that distributors and manufacturers will lose interest if you negotiate too much profit out of the sale. Never forget that their services are valuable. You may need them if you have a problem.

Make sure you have a copy of the warranty on your equipment. Read these warranties carefully. Know what part of the warranty is backed by the manufacturer and what part is backed by the distributor. What is the length of the labor warranty? What is the length of the parts warranty? On what date does the warranty begin? On what date does it end?

Quotations should specify how and when payment is to be made. In the absence of credit arrangements, equipment is usually shipped c.o.d. and the amount of the invoice (less your deposit) is collected by the delivering carrier. You will need to obtain a certified check or bank check in advance. You pay the driver when the shipment arrives.

Sometimes "sight drafts" are used to collect c.o.d. shipments. The seller ships the equipment on an order bill-of-lading consigned to the order of himself. He attaches to it a sight draft drawn on you. These papers are sent to your bank. Your bank will notify you when they arrive. You pay the sight draft and receive a "paid" bill-of-lading. When shipment arrives, you give it to the driver as evidence of payment. You acquire legal title to the equipment when the sight draft is paid.

Choose your suppliers carefully. It pays to do business with reputable companies. Check the financial strength and reputation of all suppliers you are considering as sources for equipment. There is no end to the problems caused by inept or unethical business people. <u>Being right does not guarantee justice</u>.

Coin Laundries — Road to Financial Independence

The reputation of a man is like his shadow, gigantic when it precedes him, and pigmy in its proportions when it follows.

—Alexandre de Talleyrand-Périgord

14

ESTIMATING CONSTRUCTION OR REMODELING COSTS

YOU MAY THINK that planning and building a self-service laundry requires technical training and years of experience. Nothing could be farther from the truth. Technical training and experience is helpful, but it's not as important as your ability to hire and manage the right people.

One contractor talks about the time a prospective coin laundry owner walked into his office with a piece of notebook paper in his hand. The paper contained a hand-drawn rectangle representing a coin laundry floor and a number of hand-drawn squares in the rectangle labeled "washers" and "dryers." The only instructions the contractor got were: "Here's where the machines are gonna set. You make 'em work! How much?" It was the first coin laundry for the owner and the contractor, but luckily the project was successful.

It's unwise, of course, to leave this much to chance. But don't get so bogged down in detail that nothing gets done. Somewhere between these two extremes lies the right plan of action. You must decide how involved you will be in the project. The more involved you are, the more money you will save. Involvement can take any number of forms, such as:

1. Hiring and managing a general contractor.
2. Acting as general contractor, and then hiring and managing subcontractors.
3. Doing some of the subcontract work.
4. Acting as a workman for one or more subcontractors.
5. Some combination of the above.

Many first-time laundry owners act as their own general contractors, doing part of the work themselves. Plumbing, mechanical, and electrical inspectors can be quite helpful in preventing errors. Although there is no cure for a poor location or inadequate parking, construction errors can usually be remedied without much delay or expense.

Hire a general contractor if you cannot spare the time and effort necessary to make your leasehold improvements . A qualified general contractor will provide construction blueprints, obtain the necessary building permits, select and buy the materials, schedule the work of all subcontractors, and work with the building inspectors. If you don't hire a general contractor, you must perform all of these functions yourself.

It's easy to find general contractors. The objective is to find qualified contractors to bid your job. Try to select contractors who have experience in commercial construction, particularly in the construction of coin laundries. But don't substitute experience for honesty and competence. Selecting contractors from the *Yellow Pages* or newspaper want ads is like ordering a bride by mail. It's best to develop your list from the recommendations of others.

Good sources are your landlord or owners of other coin laundries. Building department records contain names and addresses of contractors who have built coin laundries in the area. Equipment distributors or plumbing and electrical supplies houses can also be good sources of information. They are likely to supply the names of their best and most financially sound customers.

Don't consider contractors who are not bonded. Verify the performance bond with the bonding company before you award a contract. Make sure the bond is sufficient to protect you against any loss caused by your contractor.

Investigate contractors thoroughly. Ask for references and check them carefully. If a contractor can supply a long list of satisfied customers, chances are that he will satisfy you. Check credit ratings. Your bank can often be persuaded to provide them, especially if they are going to lend you the money to pay the contractors.

When dealing with small firms, particularly partnerships or proprietorships, ask the contractor for a current financial statement. A visit to the contractor's bank and to his sources of materials also proves informative. If the contractor is good, his bank and suppliers will say so with enthusiasm. If he isn't, very little will be said.

If you act as the general contractor, you will need a set of drawings to get the necessary building permit(s). Visit the building and fire departments and find out what information is required on the blueprints. There may also be other governmental agencies involved. Make sure that all governmental requirements are met before starting construction.

The cost of your drawings can range from a few dollars to thousands of dollars. This will depend on who does the drafting and how much detail is required by the municipal government. An engineering firm may charge 10 percent (or more) of the total cost of your coin laundry to supply a set of blueprints. If the law will allow it, consider buying $50 worth of drafting equipment and drawing your own blueprints. See pages 154 through 167 for sample blueprints drawn by a coin laundry owner.

Sources for drawings include:

• Engineering firm
• Engineering firm employee on his or her own time

- Landlord's construction department
- Equipment distributor
- College student draftsman
- General contractor

After you have your drawings, write a complete set of specifications for each phase of the job. Explain what you expect of each subcontractor. Each subcontractor who is to bid the job should get:

1. Invitation to bid
2. Blueprints
3. Specifications
4. Equipment specification sheets
5. Equipment installation instructions

Meet each contractor at the job site, and go over the blueprints and specifications. Make a note of any changes to the blueprints or specifications on both the contractor's copy and your's. Make sure that you both acknowledge these changes by signing your names next to each change. This will lessen the chance of a misunderstanding later.

Expect a big difference in bids. One coin laundry owner received bids from three general contractors of $47,000, $72,000 and $83,000 for the leasehold improvements. Then, disgusted with the figures, he decided to act as his own general contractor. He completed the job for just under $34,000. The plumbing bids alone had ranged from $1,800 to $28,000. The actual cost was $9,200.

If you accept an unusually low bid, you may be headed for trouble, especially in those areas that do not require government inspections, like finished carpentry. A "low ball" bid from a carpenter is almost certain to produce a store full of dimensional kindling.

If you carefully qualify each contractor before you select the ones to bid your job, you can eliminate some of the wide variations in bids. Remember, if you want the subcontractors to submit realistic bids and perform good work, you must give them accurate and detailed information. WARNING: never use a bid from a subcontractor who does not walk the job site.

Poor communication will cost you money. If changes are made after construction begins, their cost can be many times greater than if they were incorporated in the original bid. You can be sure that the contractor will compensate for being low bidder by charging high prices for changes to the contract.

If you are new at this, have your attorney draw up the "invitation-to-bid." This can protect you from a variety of abuses. Give this to the subcontractors along with copies of the blueprints, work specifications, equipment specifications, and equipment installation instructions. Your attorney should consider the following when drafting the invitation:

- Performance bond
- Time of performance
- Right to replace
- Quality of work
- Payment terms
- Pricing revisions

PERFORMANCE BOND

Require the general contractor and/or subcontractors to be bonded and to provide a copy of the bond. Specify the bond requirements in the bid invitation. Before awarding a contract, have your attorney verify that the bond is sufficient to protect your interests.

A bond can prevent liens against your property if the general contractor fails to pay the subcontractor or if subcontractors fail to pay their employees or materials suppliers. It can also pay any damages you may suffer if the contractor fails to perform as agreed in the contract.

TIME OF PERFORMANCE

Proper work scheduling is critical! You must coordinate the work of several subcontractors if the job is to be done quickly. If time limits are not specified in the contract, a contractor can delay your job indefinitely, costing you thousands of dollars.

Some contractors commonly "salt the job." They move materials onto the job site, work for one day, and then don't return for days (or weeks) while they work on other projects that have a deadline. They return to finish your job at their convenience. For this reason, *always specify time limits in the contract.*

RIGHT TO REPLACE

Make provisions in the contract for remedial action if a contractor doesn't perform according to the terms. Establish your right to hire another contractor to finish the job with increases in cost being paid by the original contractor. Also make sure that the contractor's bond provides for this.

QUALITY OF WORK

For your protection, your attorney should specify definite quality standards in the contract for all work that is to be performed. This should apply to both labor and materials.

PAYMENT TERMS

The contract should also state how and when the contractor (or subcontractors) is to be paid.

PRICING REVISIONS

No matter how carefully you plan, there are always changes. And contractors can charge shamefully high prices for these. One

Estimating Construction or Remodeling Costs

electrical contractor told a laundry owner that the cost to convert the wiring from 110-volt to 208-volt for four front-loading washers would be $975. The owner and his friend made what they called a "midnight conversion." It cost him the price of a 100-foot coil of wire, eight cans of beer, and a pizza.

Make sure your contract establishes a basis for pricing revisions. Try to limit them to the increase in cost for labor and materials. It's worth it to have a good attorney write your contract. You'll be less likely to hear: "This is extra because it's not in our agreement." or, "I planned on doing it this way, but you want it done that way. That's a lot more expensive!"—etc., etc.

The three major job classifications in the construction of self-service laundries are: plumbing (sewer, water, gas lines, fire sprinkler system), electrical, and sheet metal. You may also need to contract for work in the following areas:

- Walls (rough carpentry)
- Ceiling
- Windows
- Wallpaper, paint, stain, etc.
- Floor covering
- Cabinetwork (miscellaneous finish carpentry)

Some contractors may offer to work on an hourly basis. This means that you purchase the materials, and the contractor charges an hourly rate for labor. Other contractors may offer a "time and materials" bid, where you pay for their time and the cost of materials. Another version of this is the "cost plus" bid, where the contractor itemizes the labor, materials, and profit. In any of these cases, you don't know your cost until the job is finished.

These types of bids might be acceptable if you were highly experienced and had a long working relationship with the contractor. If you are inexperienced though, you would be wise only to accept firm, lump-sum bids.

WORKING WITH INSPECTORS

If the construction industry operated without having to meet certain standards, the result would be chaos. Millions of people would be exposed to a variety of hazards. Building and fire inspectors who enforce the building codes are there for your protection. If you do the general contracting, you will find it difficult to build a good self-service laundry without their help. They are there to make sure that your subcontractors perform quality work.

Contact the building and fire departments before planning your laundry layout. The inspectors can offer many cost-saving ideas, as well as information on the best materials and construction procedures. They will tell you what you need to get your plans approved. This will save time you spend correcting and revising your drawings.

Experienced inspectors are walking construction encyclopedias. Be honest with them. Build a good working relationship. They are your experts, working for you to keep your subcontractors honest. Their services are valuable, and they are free.

The next few pages show samples of specifications and drawings developed by a coin laundry owner and used for constructing a medium-sized self-service laundry. They are included for general information only. Since laws, code requirements, and construction procedures vary from area-to-area, these plans and specifications should not be used in whole, or in part, for planning or building any other self-service laundry.

Estimating Construction or Remodeling Costs

PLUMBING SPECIFICATIONS

1. Contractor to provide blueprints and obtain required permits.
2. All materials and material installation is to conform to all code requirements, and to the installation specifications established by the equipment manufacturers for proper operation.
3. Provide for removal on a daily basis of all trash and construction debris resulting from alteration, or construction work performed in or around the premises as specified in the contract.
4. All sewer pipe, sewer vent pipe, water lines and gas lines in the equipment room are to be installed or routed so that they are not visible.

Sewer

5. Provide for cutting and removal of existing concrete floor for installation of under-floor sewer lines. Provide for replacement of concrete, complete with wire reinforcing mesh, on suitable pneumatic tamper prepared base.
6. Provide and install sewer lines, complete with sewer vents and cleaning accesses, with all feeder sewer lines connected to the main sewer line. Provide and install stand pipes for top-loading washers that are accessible to the washer drain hoses. Connect sewer line direct to each front-loading washer.
7. Provide and install rest room sink and water closet. Connect sewer line to each fixture.
8. Provide and install 6 floor drains behind washers and 1 floor drain in water heater room. Drains to be located per attached drawing.
9. Provide and install floor, wall or overhead support attachments where required for sewer vents and sewer lines. Provide and install wall or roof jacks for all sewer vents.

10. All sewer lines and sewer vents are to be installed so that they do not obstruct or prevent installation of the other services required for the equipment.

Water

11. Provide and install all water lines to provide water in sufficient pressure and volume for proper operation of all equipment when operating simultaneously. Locate hot and cold water lines with hand operated shutoff valves within reach of each of the top-loading washer hoses. Valves to have threaded male fittings for hose attachment. Hot and cold water lines to be connected to each front-loading washer. Provide each line with a hand operated shutoff valve.

12. Provide and install all hot water lines between the water heater and the water tank, including installation of the recirculating water pump supplied with the heater. Provide hand operated shutoff valves at every water entry and exit location on water tank and water heater. Install the pressure valves supplied with heater and tank. Provide and install the blowoff lines to floor drain.

13. Provide and install hot and cold water lines to rest room sink with hand operated shutoff valves. Provide and install cold water line to water closet complete with shutoff valve.

14. Provide and connect cold water lines complete with hand operated shutoff valves to evaporative coolers. Valves to be located inside building and easily accessible.

15. Provide and install in-line water meter in utility room with meter at eye level. Provide hand operated shutoff valves at entry to and exit from meter. Meter to be installed to measure total water usage of coin laundry.

16. All valves to be high quality and subject to approval by owner.
17. Provide and install rigid glass fiber pipe insulation on all over-head cold water lines to prevent condensation. Provide and install 6-inch glass fiber bat insulation around water tank. Cover insulation with suitable wrap. Provide and install rigid glass fiber pipe insulation on all hot water lines larger than 1 inch in diameter.
18. Provide and install floor, wall or overhead support attachments for the water lines where required. All water lines are to be installed so that they do not obstruct or prevent installation of the other services required for the equipment.

Natural Gas

19. Provide and install all natural gas lines to provide natural gas in sufficient pressure and volume for proper operation of all equipment when operating simultaneously. Natural gas lines to be connected to the gas meter, clothes dryers, hot water heater and unit space heaters with a manual shutoff valve located at each appliance.
20. Provide and install floor, wall or overhead support attachments for the natural gas lines where required. All natural gas lines are to be installed so that they do not obstruct or prevent installa-tion of the other services required for the equipment.

ELECTRICAL SPECIFICATIONS

1. Contractor to provide required drawings and obtain required permits.
2. All materials and material installation is to conform to all code requirements, and to the installation specifications established by the equipment manufacturers for proper operation.
3. Provide for removal on a daily basis of all trash and construction debris resulting from alteration or construction work performed in or around the premises as specified in the contract.
4. All wiring in the equipment room to be installed or routed so that it is not visible or accessible to customers.
5. Provide and install wire conduit where required. Provide and install all floor, wall or overhead support attachments where required. Electrical wiring and accessories to be installed so as not to obstruct or prevent installation of the other services required for the equipment.
6. Contractor to provide all circuit breakers and to connect all wiring to existing electrical control panel.
7. Provide and install 208-volt single-phase electrical cords with plugs on 6 front-loading washers and 6 large-drum dryers.
8. Provide, install and connect electrical plug receptacles for each of the washers and dryers in the equipment room. Locate them within reach of the electrical service cords of the washers and dryers.
9. Provide wiring and connect hot water heater and circulating pump. Provide disconnect switch. Switch to be located on heater room wall near entry door.
10. Provide 208-volt single-phase wiring connected directly to evaporative coolers. Provide 110-volt single-phase wiring connected directly to unit heaters. Mount heater thermostats (2) in lock-boxes at locations shown on blueprints and connect to heaters. Provide and install disconnect switches for each evaporative cooler and each heater. Switches to be located in storage room.

11. Provide flex conduit with 110-volt wiring and connect to coin/bill changers.
12. Provide and install an isolated circuit for cash register with plug receptacle located behind service counter at location shown on blueprint.
13. Provide and install 110-volt plug receptacle for clock and television set at locations shown on blueprint.
14. Provide and install exterior sign electrical junction-box with 110-volt wiring. Provide and install sign disconnect switch in storage room.
15. Provide, install and connect 8 15-ampere, 110-volt double receptacle wall outlets and 2 20-ampere, 110-volt double receptacle wall outlets at locations shown on blueprints.
16. Provide and install 20 (10% of ceiling area) 2-foot by 4-foot, 4-light fluorescent tube lighting fixtures in equipment room, complete with tubes. Fixtures to be ceiling-grid drop-in type located to provide uniform lighting throughout equipment room. Provide and install 2 disconnect switches in storage room to provide 50 percent illumination and 100 percent illumination uniformly throughout equipment room.
17. Provide and install 5 light-fixture junction-boxes flush with ceiling and centered over each clothes-folding table. All junction-boxes to be wired to a disconnect switch located in storage room.
18. Provide and install a ceramic light fixture with disconnect wall-switch in both the utility room and the water heater room. Switches to be located near entry doors.
19. Provide and install a 2-foot by 4-foot, 4-light fluorescent tube lighting fixture in the storage room, complete with tubes. Fixture to be ceiling-grid drop-in type. Provide and install the disconnect switch near the storage room entry door.
20. Provide and install a fluorescent light fixture over rest room mirror, complete with tubes and disconnect switch located next to entry door.
21. Provide and install all security system wiring per vendor's plans and specifications, copy attached.

SHEET METAL SPECIFICATIONS

1. Contractor to provide required drawings and obtain required permits.
2. All materials and material installation is to conform to all code requirements, and to the installation specifications established by the equipment manufacturers for proper operation.
3. Provide for removal on a daily basis of all trash and construction debris resulting from alteration or construction work performed in or around the premises as specified in the contract.
4. All duct work in equipment room to be installed so that it is not visible.
5. Provide and install 2 water heater supply-air intake-ducts as shown in blueprints. Provide and install water heater exhaust vent as shown in blueprint.
6. Provide and install exhaust vents for 2 40,000-B.t.u., ceiling-mounted heaters.
7. Provide and install roof mounts for evaporative coolers, complete with roof flashing.
8. Provide air ducts from coolers to ceiling, 2-foot by 4-foot ceiling grid adaptor, and adjustable louvered ceiling grille. Install ducts, adaptors and grilles, and connect ducts to coolers.
9. Provide and install 32 dryer vents and 8 dryer supply-air intake-ducts for stacked dryers. Dryer vents to be 4-inch diameter aluminum with all connecting joints taped only. Vents to exit through roof in groups of 4 vents routed inside a 16-inch diameter supply-air intake-duct. Each supply-air duct to be a continuous duct from 3 inches above ceiling line to 4 inches above roof line. Provide and install 8 rain-caps over supply-air intake-ducts. Screen air intake-ducts against birds.

10. Provide and install 6 dryer vents and 6 dryer supply-air intake-ducts for 6 30-pound-capacity dryers. Dryer vents to be 8 inches in diameter with all connecting joints screwed and taped. Vents to be routed inside a 14-inch diameter supply-air intake-duct. Each supply-air duct to be a continuous duct from top of dryer to 4 inches above roof line. Provide and install 6 rain-caps over supply-air intake-ducts. Screen supply-air intake-ducts against birds.

11. All sheet metal work is to be installed so that it does not obstruct or prevent installation of the other services required for the equipment.

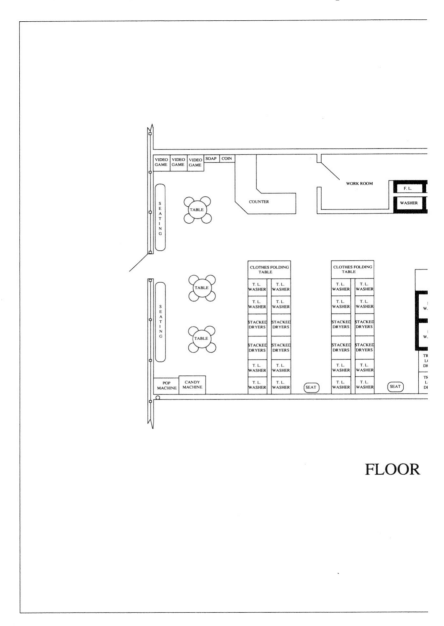

FLOOR

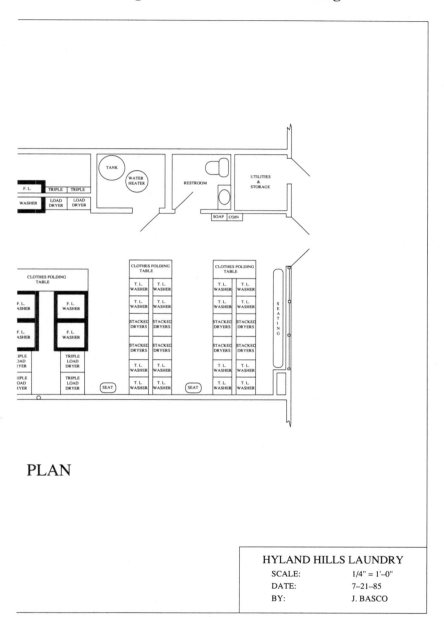

PLAN

HYLAND HILLS LAUNDRY	
SCALE:	1/4" = 1'–0"
DATE:	7–21–85
BY:	J. BASCO

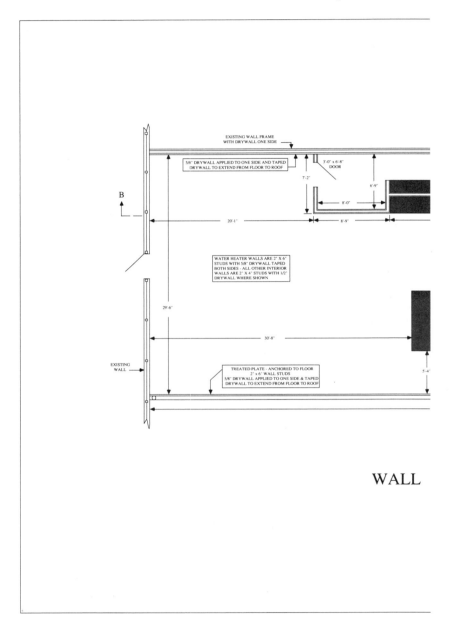

EXISTING WALL FRAME
WITH DRYWALL ONE SIDE

5/8" DRYWALL APPLIED TO ONE SIDE AND TAPED
DRYWALL TO EXTEND FROM FLOOR TO ROOF

3'-0" x 6'-8"
DOOR

7'-2"

6'-9"

B

20'-1"

8'-0"

8'-9"

WATER HEATER WALLS ARE 2" X 6"
STUDS WITH 5/8" DRYWALL TAPED
BOTH SIDES - ALL OTHER INTERIOR
WALLS ARE 2" X 4" STUDS WITH 1/2"
DRYWALL WHERE SHOWN

29'-6"

30'-8"

EXISTING
WALL

TREATED PLATE - ANCHORED TO FLOOR
2" x 6" WALL STUDS
5/8" DRYWALL APPLIED TO ONE SIDE & TAPED
DRYWALL TO EXTEND FROM FLOOR TO ROOF

5'-4"

WALL

Estimating Construction or Remodeling Costs

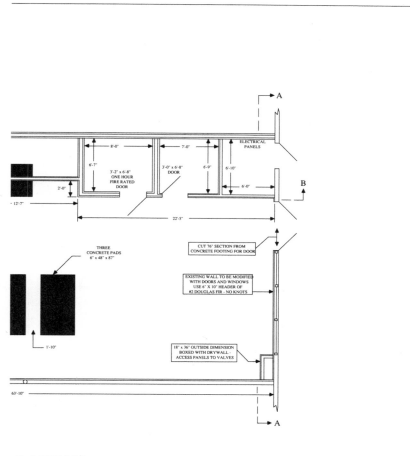

A

ELECTRICAL
PANELS

8'-0"   7'-0"

6'-7"

3'-2" x 6'-8"   3'-0" x 6-8"   6'-9"   6'-10"
ONE HOUR   DOOR
FIRE RATED
DOOR   6'-0"   B

2'-0"

- 12'-7" -

22'-5"

THREE   CUT 76" SECTION FROM
CONCRETE PADS   CONCRETE FOOTING FOR DOOR
6" x 48" x 87"

EXISTING WALL TO BE MODIFIED
WITH DOORS AND WINDOWS
USE 6" X 10" HEADER OF
#2 DOUGLAS FIR - NO KNOTS

18" x 36" OUTSIDE DIMENSION
BOXED WITH DRYWALL -
ACCESS PANELS TO VALVES

1'-10"

63'-10"

A

LAYOUT

HYLAND HILLS LAUNDRY	
SCALE:	1/4" = 1'–0"
DATE:	7–21–85
BY:	J. BASCO

157

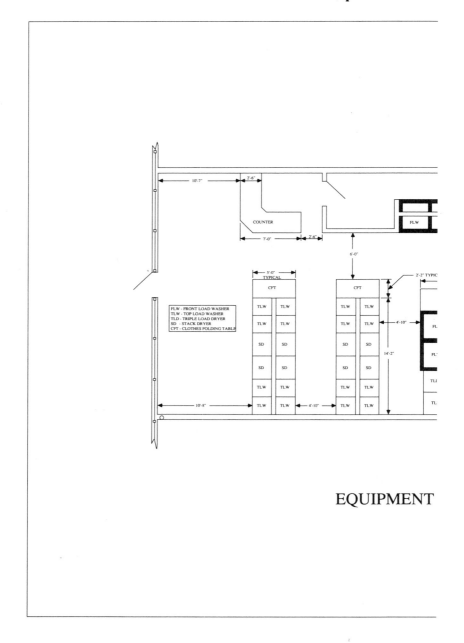

EQUIPMENT

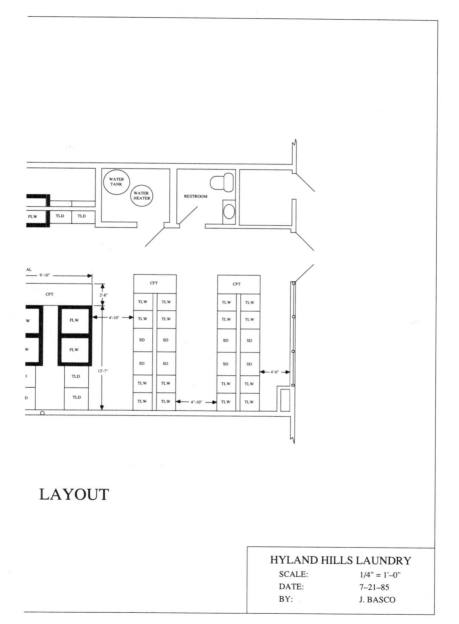

LAYOUT

HYLAND HILLS LAUNDRY

SCALE:	1/4" = 1'–0"
DATE:	7–21–85
BY:	J. BASCO

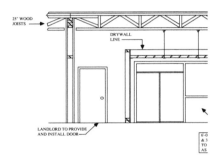

SOUTH WALL

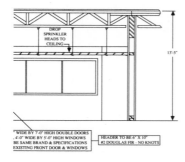

13'-5"

DROP
SPRINKLER
HEADS TO
CEILING

" WIDE BY 7'-0" HIGH DOUBLE DOORS
, 4'-0" WIDE BY 5'-0" HIGH WINDOWS
BE SAME BRAND & SPECIFICATIONS
EXISTING FRONT DOOR & WINDOWS

HEADER TO BE 6" X 10"
#2 DOUGLAS FIR - NO KNOTS

SECTION A-A

HYLAND HILLS LAUNDRY	
SCALE:	1/4" = 1'–0"
DATE:	7–21–85
BY:	J. BASCO

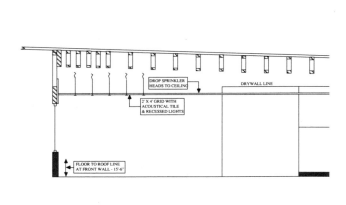

DROP SPRINKLER
HEADS TO CEILING

DRYWALL LINE

2' X 4' GRID WITH
ACOUSTICAL TILE
& RECESSED LIGHTS

FLOOR TO ROOF LINE
AT FRONT WALL - 15'-6"

EAST WALL

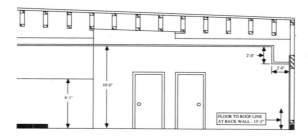

2'-0"

2'-0"

10'-0"

6'-1"

FLOOR TO ROOF LINE
AT BACK WALL - 13'-5"

SECTION B-B

HYLAND HILLS LAUNDRY	
SCALE:	1/4" = 1'–0"
DATE:	7–21–85
BY:	J. BASCO

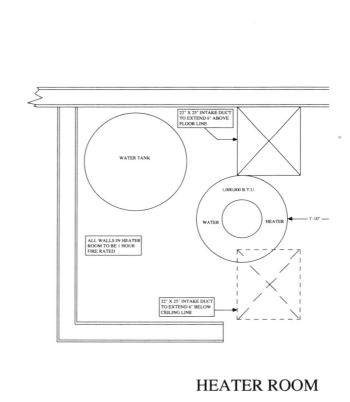

WATER TANK

22" X 25" INTAKE DUCT
TO EXTEND 6" ABOVE
FLOOR LINE

1,000,000 B.T.U.

WATER   HEATER   ← 1'-10" —

ALL WALLS IN HEATER
ROOM TO BE 1 HOUR
FIRE RATED

22" X 25" INTAKE DUCT
TO EXTEND 6" BELOW
CEILING LINE

HEATER ROOM

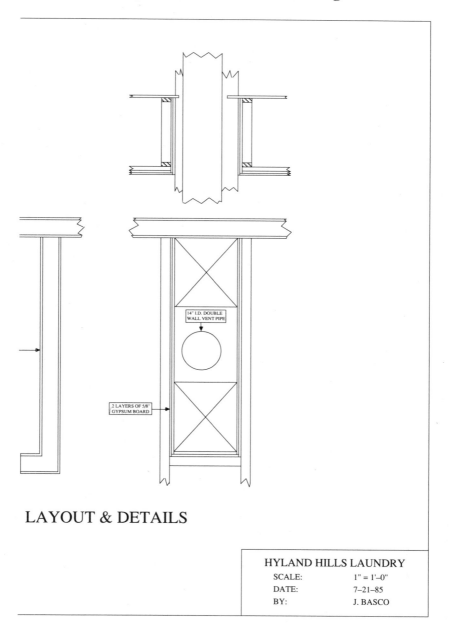

14" I.D. DOUBLE WALL VENT PIPE

.2 LAYERS OF 5/8" GYPSUM BOARD

LAYOUT & DETAILS

HYLAND HILLS LAUNDRY	
SCALE:	1" = 1'-0"
DATE:	7-21-85
BY:	J. BASCO

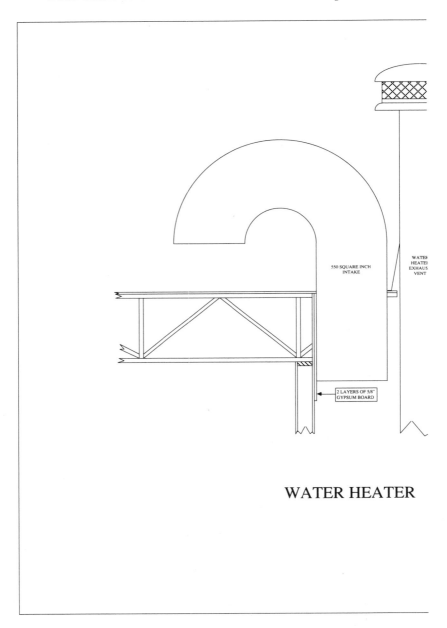

550 SQUARE INCH INTAKE

WATER HEATER EXHAUST VENT

2 LAYERS OF 5/8" GYPSUM BOARD

WATER HEATER

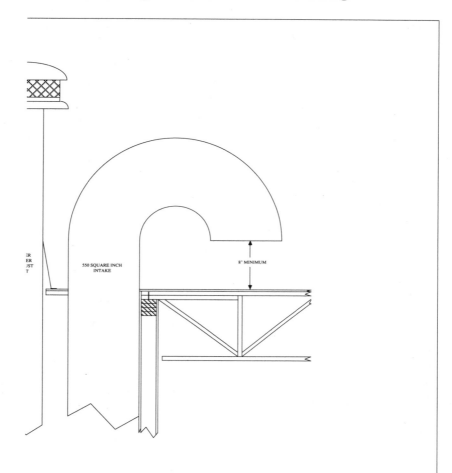

VENT & AIR INTAKE

HYLAND HILLS LAUNDRY	
SCALE:	1"= 1'–0"
DATE:	7–21–85
BY:	J. BASCO

Coin Laundries — Road to Financial Independence

> You may be whatever you resolve to be. Determine to be something in the world, and you will be something. "I cannot," never accomplished anything; "I will try," has wrought wonders.
>
> —Joel Hawes

15

DEVELOPING YOUR OPERATING PLAN

THE MOMENT OF truth has arrived. You must now make a decision to proceed with your plans or to abandon the project altogether. If you proceed, you will sign a 10-year lease, contingent on your getting adequate financing. Base your decision on an analysis of your operating plan.

This chapter shows you how to develop your operating plan. The figures in this example are for a fictitious busine ss—a 24-washer, 12-stacked dryer, unattended coin-operated laundry located in 1,200 square feet of leased space in a shopping center.

Here are the eight steps you need to take to develop your operating plan:

1. Determine the utility rates
2. Determine utility usage and cost
3. Project the equipment-use-factor
4. Establish pricing

5. Estimate sales volume
6. Determine operating expenses
7. Develop an Operating Plan Forecast
8. Develop a monthly Cash Flow Projection

Study each step carefully to make sure you understand it before going on. Each step provides you with information you need for the next step. Don't take shortcuts or you will get confused. When you have completed all eight steps, you will know the profit potential of your self-service laundry.

UTILITY RATES

Utility costs are another of your major expenses. <u>Do everything possible to hold them down</u>! Visit the customer service departments of the gas and electric companies and the municipal water and sewer departments. Determine what rate schedules are available. If there is more than one, ask the utility representative to help you figure out which is best for you. Analyze each one carefully.

For purposes of this example, let's use the following utility rates:

* <u>Natural Gas</u> — A minimum charge of $267.77 per month or a price of 46.887¢ per therm (100,000 B.t.u. or 100 cubic feet), whichever is greater. (This gas produces 1,000 B.t.u. per cubic foot.)

* <u>Water</u> — 60¢ per 100 cubic feet (748 gallons).

* <u>Sewer</u> — A flat rate of $111.00 per month.

* <u>Electricity</u> — A monthly rate based on the number of kilowatts (1,000 watts) of electricity used per hour. (This is sometimes written as kw.-hr. or kwh.) The rate is divided into summer and winter as follows:

Developing Your Operating Plan

Summer — May through Oct. — 6.030¢ per kwh
Winter — Nov. through April — 6.621¢ per kwh

UTILITY USAGE AND COST

You'll need utilities to operate your equipment and to provide lighting. The following chart lists the equipment and lighting in the laundry and shows utility needs for each:

UTILITY USAGE CHART

Item	Sewer	Water	Natural Gas	Electricity
24 Washers	X	X	X*	X
12 Stacked Dryers			X	X
Water Heater				X
Ceiling-Mounted Space Heater			X	X
Roof-Mounted Evaporative Cooler		X		X
Soft Drink Machine				X
Candy Machine				X
Coin/Bill Changer				X
15 4-Tube Ceiling Fixtures				X
Exterior Sign				X
4 60-Watt Lights				X
1 100-Watt Light				X
Television Set				X
Vacuum Cleaner				X
Clock				X

* Washers do not use natural gas, but the entire production of the water heater is used to provide hot water for the washers. The amount of gas required for the water heater depends on the amount of hot water used per washer cycle and the frequency of use.

Coin Laundries — Road to Financial Independence

Sewer

The sewer charge is a <u>fixed</u> expense—$111 per month no matter how many times the washers are used.

Water

Water is a <u>variable</u> expense. The cost will vary according to how much the washers are used. The amount of water evaporated in the evaporative cooler is too little to be important.

The specification sheets reveal that the washers use 34 gallons of water per cycle. At 60¢ per 100 cubic feet (748 gallons), the cost of the water per cycle is 2.7¢ (34 ÷ 748 • .60 = .027).

Natural Gas

Natural gas provides heat in the ceiling-mounted space-heater, heats water for the clothes washers, and provides heat for the clothes dryers. How much natural gas the space heater uses will depend primarily on:

- Outside temperature
- How well the laundry is insulated
- Thermostat setting of the heater

While it's difficult to provide an accurate cost figure for heating the laundry, you will need an estimate for your operating plan. The estimate on page 173 assumes that the building is well insulated, the winter will be cold, and the heater thermostat will be turned down each night.

A more accurate figure can be determined for the natural gas you need to heat water for the washers. You need to know the following to figure this cost (see pages 85, 92 and 93):

- Average gallons of hot water used per washer cycle
- Temperature rise of heated water
- Water heater efficiency

COST TO HEAT LAUNDRY

Maximum Gas Input Per Hour	Estimated Percentage Of Time Burner Is Cycled On Per Hour	Hours Of Operation Per Day	B.t.u. Used Per Day
40,000 B.t.u.	66-2/3 %	16 (Open)	426,667
40,000 B.t.u.	33-1/3 %	8 (Closed)	106,667
		24	533,334

$$\frac{533,334 \text{ B.t.u.}}{100,000 \text{ B.t.u.}} = 5\text{-}1/3 \text{ Therms Per Day} \cdot 46.887¢ = \$2.50$$

$2.50 = Maximum Heating Cost Per Day

For this example, use an average of 9.68 gallons of hot water per cycle and raise the water temperature 80° Fahrenheit in a water heater that is 75 percent efficient. It takes one B.t.u. to raise one pound of water one Fahrenheit degree. Water weighs 8.345 pounds per gallon. Figure the B.t.u. needed to heat the water for an average washer cycle:

$$\text{B.t.u.} = \frac{9.68 \text{ Gal.} \cdot 8.345 \text{ Lb.} \cdot 80°F.}{.75 \text{ (Heater Efficiency)}} = 8,616 \text{ B.t.u.}$$

The average cost per cycle to heat the water is:

$$\frac{8,616 \text{ B.t.u.}}{100,000 \text{ B.t.u. Per Therm}} \cdot 46.887¢ \text{ Per Therm} = 4.0¢ \text{ Per Cycle}$$

Each stacked dryer has two clothes drying chambers. Each chamber will dry one washer load of clothes. Ask the manufacturer for the following information so you can determine the average gas consumption per cycle for your dryers (see pages 85 and 86):

- The number of pounds of water remaining in the clothes at the end of the wash cycle.
- The number of cubic feet of gas the dryer needs to evaporate a pound of moisture.

Let's say the clothes washer produces a washed load of clothes that is 188 percent of its dry weight and the capacity of the washer is 8 pounds of dry clothes. In this case, the washed load will weigh 15 pounds (1.88 • 8 pounds = 15). This means that the dryer will have to evaporate 7 pounds of water. If your dryers require 2 cubic feet of gas to evaporate a pound of water, they will use 14 cubic feet of gas per washer load for drying.

Figure your cost per load as follows:

$$\frac{14 \text{ Cubic Feet}}{100 \text{ Cubic Feet}} \bullet 46.887¢ \text{ Per 100 Cubic Feet} = 6.6¢ \text{ Per Load}$$

When you figure your monthly gas cost, don't forget that you have a minimum charge of $267.77.

Electricity

Electricity is measured in watts or kilowatts (1,000 watts). Ask the manufacturers and/or distributors for the following information:

- Watts consumed per cycle to operate the washers.
- Watts required to operate the dryers for an average drying cycle. (A dryer that consumes 366 watts per hour would use approximately 213 watts per cycle if the average drying time was 35 minutes.)
- Maximum and/or average watts per hour to operate all other equipment and lights.

174

Developing Your Operating Plan

The following chart shows the electricity consumption for your laundry based on an average 30.4-day month:

ELECTRICAL USAGE CHART

Item	Watts Per Cycle	KWH Per Cycle
Washers	150	.15
Dryers	213	.213

Item	Maximum Watts Per Hour	Hours Of Operation Per Day	Total Watts Per Month (30.4 Days)	KWH Per Month
Water Heater Recirculating Pump	218	15	99,408	99.4
Evaporative Cooler	475 (Summer)	8	115,520	115.5
15 4-Tube Fixtures	2,400	16	1,167,360	1,167.4
Exterior Sign	700	15	319,200	319.2
4 60-Watt Lights*	240	24	175,104	175.1
Television Set	151	16	73,446	73.4
1 100-Watt Light	100	Neg.	–	–
Clock	Neg.	–	–	–

Item	Average Watts Per Hour	Hours Of Operation Per Day	Total Watts Per Month (30.4 Days)	KWH Per Month
Space Heater** Store Open	317 (Winter)	15	144,552	144.6
Store Closed	158 (Winter)	9	43,229	43.2
Soft Drink Machine	232	24	169,267	169.3
Candy Machine	50	24	36,480	36.5
Coin/Bill Changer	50	24	36,480	36.5
Vacuum Cleaner	Neg.	–	–	–

* One light over each clothes-folding table also used as night lights.
** Space heater estimated to be operating 2/3 of every hour that the laundry is open and 1/3 of every hour that the laundry is closed.

Coin Laundries — Road to Financial Independence

Some electricity costs are <u>fixed costs</u>; others are <u>variable costs</u>. Fixed costs are not affected by business volume. They remain basically the same from month-to-month. Any variations are caused by slight differences in summer and winter rates and the amount of cooling (or heating) required.

Determine these costs by adding the monthly kwh usage from the Electrical Usage Chart on page 175 and then multiplying this usage by the rate as follows:

FIXED COSTS FOR ELECTRICITY

Item	KWH Per Month (Summer)	KWH Per Month (Winter)
Recirculating Pump	99.4	99.4
Evaporative Cooler	115.5	0.0
15 Ceiling Lights	1,167.4	1,167.4
Exterior Sign	319.2	319.2
60-Watt Lights	175.1	175.1
Television Set	73.4	73.4
Space Heater	0.0	187.8
Soft Drink Machine	169.3	169.3
Candy Machine	36.5	36.5
Coin/Bill Changer	36.5	36.5
Total	2,192.3	2,264.6

	Average Monthly KWH Usage	Rate	Maximum Monthly Fixed Cost For Electricity
Summer	2,192.3	6.030¢	$132
Winter	2,264.6	6.621¢	$150

The monthly cost of electricity to operate your washers and dryers depends on your volume of business. This is a <u>variable cost</u>

and is shown as the cost per cycle. Following is the cost per cycle for the electricity needed to operate your washers and dryers:

	VARIABLE COSTS FOR ELECTRICITY		
	KWH	Rate	Cost Of Electricity Per Cycle
Washer	.15	6.030¢ (Summer)	.9 Cents
		6.621¢ (Winter)	1.0 Cents
Dryer	.213	6.030¢ (Summer)	1.3 Cents
		6.621¢ (Winter)	1.4 Cents

Page 178 shows a summary of all of the utility costs for your coin-operated laundry.

EQUIPMENT-USE-FACTOR

Before you can plan your budget, you first have to estimate your equipment-use-factor. This is the percentage of available cycles that the equipment averages daily. This figure is usually based on the washers. If your washers require 27 minutes per cycle, plus an additional 3 minutes to load and unload, each washer could run 30 cycles in a 15-hour day.

The equipment-use-factor for most coin laundries (see page 71) is somewhere between 8 and 33 percent. The average is approximately 17 percent. Base your estimate on your market survey.

Suppose you estimate that a 24-washer laundry operating in the market should attain an equipment-use-factor of 20 percent.

UTILITY COST SUMMARY

VARIABLE COSTS
(Shown As Costs Per Cycle)

	Water	Natural Gas	Electricity Summer & Winter		Total Summer & Winter	
Washer	2.7¢	4.0¢	.9¢ &	1.0¢	7.6¢ &	7.7¢
Dryer	–	6.6¢	1.3¢ &	1.4¢	7.9¢ &	8.0¢
Total	2.7¢	10.6¢	2.2¢ &	2.4¢	15.5¢ &	15.7¢

FIXED COSTS

Utility	Summer	Winter
Electricity – Cost Per Month (30.4 Days) For All Lights And Equipment Except Washers And Dryers	$132	$150
Natural Gas – Cost For Heating Is $2.50 Per Day Times 30.4 Days Per Month	–	$76
Sewer Charges Per Month	$111	$111

This is an average of 6 cycles per day for the washers and dryers (20% of 30 cycles). Set this as your goal in the first 18 months of operation.

Developing Your Operating Plan

PRICING

Two things determine the price you can charge for a washed load of clothes—competition and expenses. If your price is too high, you'll lose customers. If your price is too low, you won't make a profit. Establish your pricing by using this guideline:

<u>Monthly gross receipts from the washers and dryers should equal or exceed four times monthly rent and five times monthly utility expenses.</u>

In other words, your rent should not be more than 25 percent of washer/dryer receipts. Total utility costs should not be more than 20 percent of washers/dryer receipts. If your price is structured according to these two major expenses, the other expense-to-revenue ratios should be in line for a well-managed laundry.

Assume that your laundry has 24 washers, 12 stacked dryers (24 drying chambers), and rent of $1,100 per month (including all rent-related expenses payable to the landlord). The Price Analysis Chart on page 180 shows you how to determine pricing.

Here's how each of the figures was determined. Refer to the Utility Cost Summary on page 178. The 15.7¢ cost per cycle to operate a washer/dryer pair was based on the winter rate shown in the summary. The other utility costs were taken right from this summary. To be conservative, winter rates and winter utility consumption figures were used.

According to the two formulae, the chart clearly indicates that at an average of 4 cycles per day per machine, the price per laundry pair should be $1.50. At an average of 5 or 6 cycles per day, the price should be $1.25. At 7 cycles per day, $1.00 per washed and dried load would satisfy an average of the two formulae.

Now apply your common sense. Look at the difference in total revenue between 6 cycles at $1.25 and 7 cycles at $1.00. Why suffer the wear and tear on your equipment for less money? The only reason to charge the lower price is to draw enough additional customers to substantially increase revenue. This is not likely.

PRICE ANALYSIS CHART

	Average Number Of Cycles Per Day For Each Washer And Dryer			
	4 Cycles	5 Cycles	6 Cycles	7 Cycles
Monthly Cost Of Water, Gas And Electricity To Operate The Washers And Dryers*	$458	$573	$687	$802
Monthly Sewer Charge	111	111	111	111
Monthly Cost Of Natural Gas To Run Space Heater	76	76	76	76
Monthly Cost Of Electricity For Lights And All Equipment Except Washers And Dryers	150	150	150	150
Total Monthly Utilities Cost	$795	$910	$1,024	$1,139
Total Monthly Utility Cost Times 5	$3,975	$4,550	$5,120	$5,695
Monthly Rent Times 4	$4,400	$4,400	$4,400	$4,400

Monthly Gross Revenue At:**

Wash	Dry	Total				
$1.00	75¢	$1.75	$5,107	$6,384	$7,661	$8,938
75¢	75¢	$1.50	$4,378	$5,472	$6,566	$7,661
75¢	50¢	$1.25	$3,648	$4,560	$5,472	$6,384
50¢	50¢	$1.00	$2,918	$3,648	$4,378	$5,107

* 15.7¢ (Utility Costs To Operate A Washer And Dryer) • 24 (Washer Dryer Pairs) • Average Of 30.4 Days Per Month • Average Number Of Cycles

** Revenue Per Washer And Dryer Cycle • Average Number Of Cycles Per Day • 24 Laundry Pairs • Average Of 30.4 Days Per Month

Developing Your Operating Plan

Consider this:

- It takes approximately 8 cycles per day to justify the lower price. Eight cycles per day is a 27 percent use-factor. This approaches the maximum volume you can handle.
- The monthly difference between 6 and 8 cycles per day is 1,459 cycles. It's not likely that a 25¢ difference per load would produce 1,459 more loads per month. At an average of 3 loads per week per customer, you need 112 more customers. Your market survey will tell you whether this is possible.
- Additional promotion and careful management could increase the cycles from 6 to 6.5 at the $1.25 price with only a slight increase in costs. This would generate more revenue than 8 cycles at $1.00 per load.

Now decide if your 75¢-wash and 50¢-dry can compete with the other coin laundries in your market. Remember, you must also compete with the apartment house laundries. If you are not competitive, you can't expect to achieve an equipment-use-factor of 20 percent, your goal for this coin laundry.

SALES VOLUME PROJECTION

You probably won't achieve your volume potential in the first few months of operation, and probably not in the first year. Some coin laundries take several years to reach the volume for which they were designed. Other laundries never achieve their planned equipment-use-factor because of an inaccurate market survey, changing market conditions, or plain bad management.

It takes time to build sales volume. People are creatures of habit. Their habits can be changed, but not overnight. Since there is no known formula for figuring your rate of sales volume increase, your market survey (Chapter 7) combined with a good advertising program (Chapter 19) must stand as the basis for your projections.

181

Coin Laundries — Road to Financial Independence

Look at this 18-month projection of growth and revenue for our coin-operated laundry:

	Month	Days	Average Cycles Per Laundry Pair Per Day	Price Per Washed & Dried Load	Monthly Revenue From Washers & Dryers*
1	June	30	1.00	$.50	$360
2	July	31	3.11	.50	1,157
3	Aug.	31	4.67	.50	1,737
4	Sept.	30	3.11	1.25	2,799
5	Oct.	31	2.83	1.25	2,632
6	Nov.	30	2.91	1.25	2,619
7	Dec.	31	3.05	1.25	2,836
8	Jan.	31	3.32	1.25	3,088
9	Feb.	28	3.75	1.25	3,150
10	Mar.	31	4.15	1.25	3,860
11	April	30	4.55	1.25	4,095
12	May	31	4.91	1.25	4,566
13	June	30	5.24	1.25	4,716
14	July	31	5.51	1.25	5,124
15	Aug.	31	5.68	1.25	5,282
16	Sept.	30	5.81	1.25	5,229
17	Oct.	31	5.92	1.25	5,506
18	Nov.	30	6.00	1.25	5,400

PROJECTED GROWTH PATTERN

* Days • Cycles • 24 Pair • Price = Monthly Revenue From Washers and Dryers

Developing Your Operating Plan

For the first three months of operation, you charge 25¢ per wash and 25¢ per dry to draw prospective customers. Customers who use your laundry three or four times are likely to develop a habit. Many will continue to come back after you raise your prices.

When you raise prices after 90 days, price shock takes effect. Machine use will probably decline for the next three months. Gradually it will increase as many former customers return and new customers are added through word-of-mouth and your promotional programs.

Don't be discouraged by a big reduction in customers after you raise your prices. Many customers resist this increase. They go back to dingy apartment house laundries or to other self-service coin-operated laundries. Many of these customers will return if your prices are competitive and if you maintain a clean, well-managed laundry.

If those customers had not been enticed to your new laundry in the first place, they would not be familiar with your new machines. They would not have experienced the clean, comfortable surroundings and the convenient layout. What reason would they have to change their habits and try your new laundry?

Look at Month 4 in the Projected Growth Pattern Chart. Revenue increases substantially because you increase prices but the cycles drop as customers begin to learn of the increase. Both cycles and revenue drop in Month 5 as more customers learn of the increase. Beyond Month 5, the trend is reversed. There is a steady increase in average cycles per day. (When comparing monthly revenue, remember that the number of days in the month affects the total.)

In addition to revenue from washers and dryers, you'll make money from the sale of laundry aids, soft drinks, and snacks. This figure is directly affected by your volume of laundry business. The more people you have in the laundry, the more you will sell from the vending machines.

You can estimate vending machine revenue as a percentage of revenue generated by the washers and dryers. When you do this, compute the revenue from the washers and dryers at $1.25 per load, not 50¢ per load for the first three months, or the vending machine revenue will be grossly understated.

These percentages will be used later in this chapter to get an estimate for vending machine revenue for the Operating Plan Forecast:

Item		Percent Of Washer & Dryer Volume
Soft Drink	—	5.0%
Snacks	—	4.0%
Laundry Aids	—	3.5%

OPERATING EXPENSES

If your Operating Plan Forecast is to be accurate, you must carefully estimate all operating costs. Important decisions depend on the Operating Plan Forecast and the Cash Flow Projection, including whether to proceed with the business or abandon it entirely. Your figures must be accurate.

Cost of Goods Sold

To compute the cost of the items in your soft drink, candy and soap vending machines, figure your cost as a percentage of the selling price. (You will use these percentages when you compute the cost of goods sold in your Operating Plan Forecast.)

For example, you decide to vend cans of soft drink at 55¢ per can. This is a total of $13.20 per case (24 cans • 55¢). You find that local discount outlets offer soft drink at $8.39 per case. Determine the percentage by dividing the cost by the selling price ($8.39 cost ÷ $13.20 price = .6356 or 63.56%). If you multiply your estimated monthly soft drink sales by 63.56%, you get the cost of the soft drinks that you sold for the month.

You'll use the following percentages later in this chapter when you compute the "cost of goods sold" in the Operating Plan Forecast:

Developing Your Operating Plan

Soft Drinks	—	63.56%
Candy	—	80%
Laundry Aids	—	50%

Rent

See pages 116 through 119 for a detailed explanation of rent and related expenses that you may have to pay to your landlord. For this laundry, rent is $10.00 per square foot of space, per year. This is a total annual expense of $12,000 for the 1,200 square-foot store. Additional charges levied by the landlord total $100 per month. The total rent expense is $1,100 per month.

Utilities

Let's develop a chart to show the total monthly utility costs for the first 18 months of operation for use in your Operating Plan Forecast. Refer back to the Utility Cost Summary on page 178 for your utility expense figures. The Projected Growth Pattern Chart on page 182 will provide the estimated average monthly cycles for your washers and dryers. Using this information, develop the chart on page 186.

You compute natural gas costs by multiplying the number of days in the month by the average cycles per day times 24 laundry pair times 10.6¢. The Utility Cost Summary shows 10.6¢ as the cost of the gas required to heat the dryers and to heat water for the washers.

The cost of gas for heating the store is estimated. When you figured your natural gas usage (pages 172 and 173), you determined the <u>maximum</u> heating cost to be $2.50 per day. With this in mind, you will estimate the monthly heating costs.

In Month 5, the cost of gas for the washers and dryers is $223.19 (31 days • 2.83 cycles • 24 pair • 10.6¢). When you add this to your $25.00 estimated heating cost, you get a total gas cost of $248.19. Remember, your gas bill is subject to a minimum monthly charge of $267.77, a difference of $19.58. Add $19.58 to

UTILITY EXPENSES

Month		Days	Average Cycles Per Day Per Machine	Natural Gas	Estimated Gas Cost For Heating	Electricity	Water	Sewer	Total
1	June	30	1.00	$267.77	0.00	$147.84	$19.44	$111.00	$546.05
2	July	31	3.11	267.77	0.00	182.90	62.47	111.00	624.14
3	Aug.	31	4.67	368.29	0.00	208.44	93.81	111.00	781.54
4	Sept.	30	3.11	267.77	0.00	181.26	60.46	111.00	620.49
5	Oct.	31	2.83	242.77	25.00	178.32	56.85	111.00	613.94
6	Nov.	30	2.91	222.09	50.00	200.28	56.57	111.00	639.94
7	Dec.	31	3.05	240.54	76.00	204.46	61.27	111.00	693.27
8	Jan.	31	3.32	261.83	76.00	209.28	66.69	111.00	724.80
9	Feb.	28	3.75	267.12	76.00	210.48	68.04	111.00	732.64
10	Mar.	31	4.15	327.29	60.00	224.10	83.37	111.00	805.76
11	April	30	4.55	347.26	50.00	228.62	88.45	111.00	825.33
12	May	31	4.91	387.22	25.00	212.37	98.63	111.00	834.22
13	June	30	5.24	399.92	0.00	215.00	101.87	111.00	827.79
14	July	31	5.51	434.54	0.00	222.19	110.68	111.00	878.41
15	Aug.	31	5.68	447.95	0.00	224.97	114.10	111.00	898.02
16	Sept.	30	5.81	443.42	0.00	224.03	112.95	111.00	891.40
17	Oct.	31	5.92	466.87	25.00	228.90	118.92	111.00	950.69
18	Nov.	30	6.00	457.92	50.00	253.68	116.64	111.00	989.24

$223.19 and use $248.19 in the "natural gas" column. You need to stay sharp when working with these figures!

You calculated electrical costs by multiplying the number of days in the month by the cycles per day times 24 laundry pair. You multiplied the result by the electricity cost per cycle of 2.2¢ (summer) or 2.4¢ (winter) taken from the Utility Cost Summary. Now add the fixed electrical cost of $132 (summer) or $150 (winter) to get the total cost of electricity for the month.

According to the Utility Cost Summary, your water will cost 2.7¢ per washer cycle. To get your monthly water cost, multiply the number of days in the month by the average cycles per day times 24 washers times 2.7¢. Your sewer charges are a flat rate of $111.00 per month.

Depreciation

Depreciation is the dollar rate at which the value of your coin laundry will decline due to wear and tear or obsolescence. This expense must be offset by profits. Your total depreciation is the original cost to build your laundry plus the cost of all improvements minus the salvage value (equipment only) at the end of the lease period. This figure divided by the number of months in the lease (including options) is your monthly depreciation expense.

The depreciation used in the Operating Plan Forecast is based on the "straight line" method discussed on pages 39 and 40. Here's how to establish this depreciation:

- Equipment — Purchase price (including freight and installation costs) minus salvage value divided by the estimated number of months of useful life.
- Plumbing, Electrical and Sheet Metal Work — Cost divided by the total number of months in the lease (including the total number of months for which you have options to renew).
- Carpentry and Other Leasehold Improvements — Cost divided by the estimated number of months of useful life. Useful life must not be greater than the total number of months in the lease (including option periods).

What would be the "straight line" monthly depreciation for 24 washers costing $18,000 including freight and installation? Using a salvage value of $3,600 and a useful life of 7 years, depreciation would be $171 per month ($18,000 - $3,600 ÷ 84 months).

Carefully consider the useful life for all items. Refer to your equipment and construction estimates, and separate the items according to their life expectancy. A wall will last for the life of your lease, but what about the finish? You may need to paint or to replace wallpaper every three to four years. If you don't consider this when you calculate depreciation for your Operating Plan Forecast, the net profit figures will be wrong.

Don't confuse the depreciation described in this chapter with the depreciation rates allowed as a business expense for tax purposes. Depreciation schedules for tax purposes are fixed by law. Your accountant will use the Federal, state and/or local schedules at tax time.

Determine the monthly depreciation for every leasehold improvement and each piece of equipment in your laundry. Assume that the monthly total is $715. Use this figure in your Operating Plan Forecast.

Interest

The cost of money you borrow to build, buy, or operate your business is an expense. If you borrow $75,000 for 5 years at an interest rate of 12 percent, your monthly payment is $1,668.34. Part of this payment is interest and part is principal. Only the interest is an expense. Your bank can supply you with a break-down showing the interest portion of each payment. Or you can calculate it yourself.

Let's say the annual interest rate is 12 percent or 1 percent per month on the balance of the loan. One percent times $75,000 equals $750 (interest). This leaves $918.34 (principal) of the $1,668.34 payment, which reduces your loan balance to $74,081.66. One percent of 74,081.66 is $740.82 (interest), which leaves $927.52 (principal) to reduce the loan balance, and so on. These calculations result in the following chart:

Month	Total Payment	Interest	Principal Payment	Principal Balance
				$75,000.00
1	$1,668.34	$750.00	$918.34	74,081.66
2	1,668.34	740.82	927.52	73,154.14
3	1,668.34	731.54	936.80	72,217.34
4	————————————Etc.————————			

Developing Your Operating Plan

Maintenance and Repair

Your new equipment is covered by a warranty, but there are always some items that are excluded, such as drive belts, bearing oil, etc. Estimate the average monthly maintenance/repair expenses for a given time period, such as a year. Assume that you estimate these expenses at $50 per month for the first 12 months. You can then increase this average to $75 per month when some of the warranties start to expire. Use these figures in your Operating Plan Forecast.

Operating Supplies

These expenses include cleaning compounds, light bulbs, vacuum cleaner bags, and other items that are used in the daily operation of your coin laundry. Estimate these expenses, and show them as a monthly average in your Operating Plan Forecast.

Insurance

The type and amount of insurance coverage depends on your needs. At the very least, you will need coverage for fire and public liability. Your insurance agent can supply prices and information on available business insurance packages. Make sure you purchase your insurance before you begin construction.

Advertising

For this example, half of the washers in this laundry are ticket-operated rather than coin-operated washers. You plan to hand-distribute 2,000 free tickets monthly to the apartments in your area for the first 18 months. The tickets are attached to a 3½-inch by 5-inch printed card. After Month 3, you plan to hand out approximately 200 free wash tickets monthly to new coin laundry customers as an inducement to return. (See page 237.)

You plan to spend $75.00 per month for the first 3 months and increase to $95.00 per month after the 3rd month. A breakdown of your advertising costs is shown on page 190.

ESTIMATED ADVERTISING EXPENSES

2,000 Tickets	—	$50.00
2,000 Printed 3-1/2" By 5" Cards	—	13.00
160 Washes (8% Projected Return) @ 7.7¢ Cost	—	12.00
Total	—	$75.00
200 Free Tickets	—	$5.00
200 Free Washes @ 7.7¢ Cost	—	15.00
Total	—	$20.00

Taxes

Your laundry has been assessed $1,600 in property taxes for the first year. These taxes will be due in Month 13 of operation. Plan a monthly tax escrow of $133 per month during the first year to pay these taxes. Property taxes for the second year are estimated at $1,200. This reduces your escrow to $100 per month beginning with Month 13 of operation.

Miscellaneous

Give your best estimate of all minor monthly expenses not listed in the above categories. This category is a "catch-all" and so the amounts should be small.

Developing Your Operating Plan

OPERATING PLAN FORECAST

You now have all the revenue and expense estimates you need for your Operating Plan Forecast. The Operating Plan Forecast on pages 192 and 193 has been developed from the estimates in this chapter.

Your Operating Plan Forecast shows that your business will be operating at a loss for the first nine months. During Month 10, you will make a small profit. Your monthly profit continues to increase through Month 18.

You will break even between Months 9 and 10. If you refer back the the Projected Growth Pattern (page 182), you will see that the washers and dryers must average about 4 cycles per day for you to break even. This is an equipment-use-factor of 13 percent (4 ÷ 30).

At this point, carefully review your market survey. Make sure that your potential customer base is sufficient to guarantee your planned equipment-use-factor of 20 percent. This is an average of 6 cycles per day for each laundry pair.

This is not the time to make a mistake. If you aren't sure that your market will provide an equipment-use-factor of 20 percent, take the following steps:

1. Survey your market again. Make sure you fully understand it.
2. Resize your coin laundry to fit your market.
3. Develop the Operating Plan Forecast for the resized coin laundry, carefully checking all figures.

Don't kid yourself by trying to make the market potential fit your laundry. You will go broke! The key to success is making your laundry fit the market potential. If your profit isn't big

OPERATING PLAN

	JUNE 1	JULY 2	AUG. 3	SEPT. 4	OCT. 5	NOV. 6	DEC. 7	JAN. 8
Revenue								
Washers & Dryers	$360	$1,157	$1,737	$2,799	$2,632	$2,619	$2,836	$3,088
Soft Drink Sales	45	145	217	140	132	131	142	154
Snack Sales	36	116	174	112	105	105	113	124
Laundry Aids	31	101	152	98	92	92	99	108
Total Revenue	$472	$1,519	$2,280	$3,149	$2,961	$2,947	$3,190	$3,474
Cost of Goods Sold								
Soft Drink	$29	$92	$138	$89	$84	$83	$90	$98
Snacks	29	93	139	90	84	84	90	99
Laundry Aids	15	50	76	49	46	46	49	54
Total Cost	$73	$235	$353	$228	$214	$213	$229	$251
Gross Profit	$399	$1,284	$1,927	$2,921	$2,747	$2,734	$2,961	$3,223
Expenses								
Rent	$1,100	$1,100	$1,100	$1,100	$1,100	$1,100	$1,100	$1,100
Utilities	546	624	782	620	614	640	693	725
Depreciation	715	715	715	715	715	715	715	715
Interest	750	741	731	722	713	703	693	684
Maintenance	50	50	50	50	50	50	50	50
Operating Supplies	25	25	25	25	25	25	25	25
Insurance	100	100	100	100	100	100	100	100
Advertising	75	75	75	95	95	95	95	95
Taxes	133	133	133	133	133	133	133	133
Miscellaneous	75	75	75	75	75	75	75	75
Total Expenses	$3,569	$3,638	$3,786	$3,635	$3,620	$3,636	$3,679	$3,702
Net Profit	($3,170)	($2,354)	($1,859)	($714)	($873)	($902)	($718)	($479)

enough, reduce your costs or abandon the market and look elsewhere. ***You get rich by owning a few highly profitable self-service laundries, not by struggling along with marginal businesses!***

CASH FLOW PROJECTION

Businesses fail because entrepreneurs don't watch their cash flow. Your Operating Plan Forecast shows that your laundry will eventually make a good profit. It does <u>not</u> tell you how much

FORECAST

	Feb. 9	Mar. 10	April 11	May 12	June 13	July 14	Aug. 15	Sept. 16	Oct. 17	Nov. 18	Total
	$3,150	$3,860	$4,095	$4,566	$4,716	$5,124	$5,282	$5,229	$5,506	$5,400	$64,156
	157	193	205	228	236	256	264	261	275	270	3,451
	126	154	164	183	189	205	211	209	220	216	2,762
	110	135	143	160	165	179	185	183	193	189	2,415
	$3,543	$4,342	$4,607	$5,137	$5,306	$5,764	$5,942	$5,882	$6,194	$6,075	$72,784
	$100	$123	$130	$145	$150	$163	$168	$166	$175	$172	$2,195
	101	123	131	146	151	164	169	167	176	173	2,209
	55	67	71	80	82	89	92	91	96	94	1,202
	$256	$313	$332	$371	$383	$416	$429	$424	$447	$439	$5,606
	$3,287	$4,029	$4,275	$4,766	$4,923	$5,348	$5,513	$5,458	$5,747	$5,636	$67,178
	$1,100	$1,100	$1,100	$1,100	$1,100	$1,100	$1,100	$1,100	$1,100	$1,100	$19,800
	733	806	825	834	828	878	898	891	951	989	13,877
	715	715	715	715	715	715	715	715	715	715	12,870
	674	664	654	644	633	623	613	602	591	581	12,016
	50	50	50	50	75	75	75	75	75	75	1,050
	25	25	25	25	25	25	25	25	25	25	450
	100	100	100	100	100	100	100	100	100	100	1,800
	95	95	95	95	95	95	95	95	95	95	1,650
	133	133	133	133	100	100	100	100	100	100	2,196
	75	75	75	75	75	75	75	75	75	75	1,350
	$3,700	$3,763	$3,772	$3,771	$3,746	$3,786	$3,796	$3,778	$3,827	$3,855	$67,059
	($413)	$266	$503	$995	$1,177	$1,562	$1,717	$1,680	$1,920	$1,781	$119

money you need to <u>start</u> your business. The Cash Flow Projection does.

You already know the cost to build your self-service laundry. You have construction bids from subcontractors and bids on the equipment from distributors and manufacturers. So how much cash do you need?

Assume you find that the total cost to build your laundry is $84,000, including construction and equipment. Your next step is to find out the amount of cash you need to start your laundry and keep it operating until it is profitable. Pages 194 and 195 show your Cash Flow Projection for the first 18 months of operation.

Coin Laundries — Road to Financial Independence

You will have a number of pre-start-up expenses, expenses that require payment before you open for business. This includes the deposit and the first month advance rent you must pay to the landlord. The estimated rent-related charges of $100 per month do not begin until Month 2 of operation.

You need deposits totalling $478 for the utility companies prior to getting service. You will also need an initial stock of operating supplies at an estimated cost of $100. You will purchase

CASH FLOW

	Prior To Start-Up	June 1	July 2	Aug. 3	Sept. 4	Oct. 5	Nov. 6	Dec. 7
Beginning Cash Balance								
Cash On Hand	$0	$1,077	$837	$904	$956	$844	$864	$845
Cash Sales	0	472	1,519	2,280	3,149	2,961	2,947	3,190
Cash Injection	5,000	3,000	2,500	2,000	700	1,000	1,000	800
Total Cash Available	$5,000	$4,549	$4,856	$5,184	$4,805	$4,805	$4,811	$4,835
Cash Paid Out								
Items For Resale	$0	$73	$235	$353	$228	$214	$213	$229
Rent	2,000	1,100	1,100	1,100	1,100	1,100	1,100	1,100
Utilities	478	546	624	782	620	614	640	693
Interest	0	750	741	731	722	713	703	693
Maintenance	0	50	50	50	50	50	50	50
Operating Supplies	100	25	25	25	25	25	25	25
Insurance	225	100	100	100	100	100	100	100
Advertising	50	75	75	75	95	95	95	95
Loan Principal	0	918	927	937	946	955	965	975
Owner's Withdrawal	0	0	0	0	0	0	0	0
Property Taxes	0	0	0	0	0	0	0	0
Miscellaneous*	1,070	75	75	75	75	75	75	75
Total Cash Paid Out	$3,923	$3,712	$3,952	$4,228	$3,961	$3,941	$3,966	$4,035
Ending Cash Balance	$1,077	$837	$904	$956	$844	$864	$845	$800
Other Data–Accumulated:								
Depreciation	$0	$715	$1,430	$2,145	$2,860	$3,575	$4,290	$5,005
Property Tax Liability	$0	$133	$266	$399	$532	$665	$798	$931

*Miscellaneous Pre-Start-Up Expenses Include:

Coin To Stock Coin/Bill Changer	–	$500
Legal Fees	–	400
Loan Costs	–	60
Business License	–	35
Other	–	75
Total		$1,070

194

Developing Your Operating Plan

insurance prior to construction at a cost of $225, and $50 for window signs announcing "a new coin laundry coming soon at this location." Miscellaneous pre-start-up expenses are explained in detail on the Cash Flow Projection.

The ending cash balances in the Cash Flow Projection might scare the owners of some businesses. But for a coin laundry, these balances are sufficient because there are no accounts receivable and no payroll, and the equipment generates new cash hourly.

PROJECTION

	Jan. 8	Feb. 9	Mar. 10	April 11	May 12	June 13	July 14	Aug. 15	Sept 16	Oct. 17	Nov 18	Total
	$800	$885	$826	$936	$1,273	$2,092	$824	$806	$808	$812	$820	$17,209
	3,474	3,543	4,342	4,607	5,137	5,306	5,764	5,942	5,882	6,194	6,075	72,784
	700	500	0	0	0	0	0	0	0	0	0	17,200
	$4,974	$4,928	$5,168	$5,543	$6,410	$7,398	$6,588	$6,748	$6,690	$7,006	$6,895	$107,193
	$251	$256	$313	$332	$371	$383	$416	$429	$424	$447	$439	$5,606
	1,100	1,100	1,100	1,100	1,100	1,100	1,100	1,100	1,100	1,100	1,100	21,800
	725	733	806	825	834	828	878	898	891	951	989	14,355
	684	674	664	654	644	633	623	613	602	591	581	12,016
	50	50	50	50	50	75	75	75	75	75	75	1,050
	25	25	25	25	25	25	25	25	25	25	25	550
	100	100	100	100	100	100	100	100	100	100	100	2,025
	95	95	95	95	95	95	95	95	95	95	95	1,700
	984	994	1,004	1,014	1,024	1,035	1,045	1,055	1,066	1,077	1,087	18,008
	0	0	0	0	0	625	1,350	1,475	1,425	1,650	1,525	8,050
	0	0	0	0	0	1,600	0	0	0	0	0	1,600
	75	75	75	75	75	75	75	75	75	75	75	2,420
	$4,089	$4,102	$4,232	$4,270	$4,318	$6,574	$5,782	$5,940	$5,878	$6,186	$6,091	$89,180
	$885	$826	$936	$1,273	$2,092	$824	$806	$808	$812	$820	$804	$18,013
	$5,720	$6,435	$7,150	$7,865	$8,580	$9,295	$10,010	$10,725	$11,440	$12,155	$12,870	
	$1,064	$1,197	$1,330	$1,463	$1,600	$100	$200	$300	$400	$500	$600	

Coin Laundries — Road to Financial Independence

The Cash Flow Projection shows you will need to make cash injections (preferably from an interest bearing account) of $17,200 through Month 9 of operation. Added to $84,000 to build the coin laundry, this is a total of $101,200. Your loan will provide $75,000, leaving $26,200 you will need in cash.

You can see why businesses fail. <u>People don't plan to fail. They fail because they don't plan.</u> Your Operating Plan Forecast and Cash Flow Projection take away the guesswork. They are management tools that help you make good management decisions and increase your chances of success.

AVERAGE MONTHLY CASH FLOW PROJECTION

The Cash Flow Projection gives you an estimated monthly cash return for the first 18 months, but what about the long term? How much cash can you expect each month <u>before</u> your loan is paid off? How much will you get <u>after</u> you pay off the loan? For answers to these questions, you need an Average Monthly Cash Flow Projection.

This projection tells you the average monthly cash flow, based on the projected equipment-use-factor of 20 percent (an average of six cycles per day per machine) for your coin laundry. You need one for the months prior to loan payoff and one for the months after loan payoff.

Page 197 shows an Average Monthly Cash Flow Projection for this laundry. Here's how to determine the figures:

Average Monthly Cash Sales

This includes revenue generated by the washers and dryers and by the vending machines. Revenue from washers and dryers is based on 6 cycles per day at $1.25 per load for an average month of 30.4 days (6 cycles • 24 pair • 30.4 days • $1.25 = $5,472).

Soft drink sales are estimated at 5 percent of washer-dryer volume (.05 • $5,472 = $274), candy and snack sales are estimated at 4 percent of washer-dryer volume (.04 • $5,472 = $219), and laundry additive sales are estimated at 3.5 percent of washer-dryer

Developing Your Operating Plan

AVERAGE MONTHLY CASH FLOW PROJECTION

	For Months 19 Through 60	After Month 60
Beginning Cash Balance:		
Cash On Hand	$850	$850
Cash Sales	6,157	6,157
Cash Injection	0	0
Total Cash Available	$7,007	$7,007
Cash Paid Out:		
Items For Resale	$445	$445
Rent	1,100	1,100
Utilities	972	972
Interest	311	0
Maintenance	96	110
Operating Supplies	25	25
Insurance	125	125
Advertising	95	95
Loan Principal	1,357	0
Owner's Withdrawal	1,477	3,143
Property Taxes	79	67
Miscellaneous	75	75
Total Cash Paid Out	$6,157	$6,157
Ending Cash Balance	$850	$850
Other Data:		
Depreciation Rate	$715	$715
Property Tax Liability	0	0

volume (.035 • $5,472 = $192). Total vending revenue comes to $685. Add this to the washer-dryer revenue and you get average monthly cash sales of $6,157.

Items for Resale

Here's the cost of the items for resale: (See pages 184 and 185.)

Soft Drink	–	63.5%	Of	$274	Sales	= $174	Cost
Snacks	–	80%	Of	219	Sales	= 175	Cost
Laundry Aids	–	50%	Of	192	Sales	= 96	Cost
Total				$685		$445	

Utilities

Getting a monthly average for utility costs is a bit harder. First, figure your annual utility costs and get a total. Next, divide the total by 12 (months) to get your average monthly utility costs. Most of your figures will come from the Utility Cost Summary on page 178. Here are the calculations for this example:

- Estimated Annual Heating Costs — Refer to your "Utility Expenses" chart on page 186. Add Months 5 through 12. Total estimated heating cost = $438.
- Natural Gas to Heat Water and Operate Dryers — A total of 52,560 washed and dried loads per year (24 pair • 6 cycles • 365 days) times 10.6¢ per load = $5,571.
- Electricity to Operate Equipment During Summer — A total of 184 days in the months of May through October times 6 cycles times 24 pair times 2.2¢ per washed and dried load = $583.
- Electricity to Operate Equipment During Winter — A total of 181 days times 6 cycles times 24 pair times 2.4¢ per washed and dried load = $626.
- Fixed Cost of Electricity During Summer — Six months times $132 = $792.
- Fixed Cost of Electricity During Winter — Six months times $150 = $900.
- Water Cost — A total of 52,560 washer cycles per year times 2.7¢ per cycle = $1,419.

- <u>Sewer Cost</u> — A monthly charge of $111 times 12 months = $1,332.

Your total estimated annual utility expenses come to $11,661, which is an average of $972 per month.

Interest

Here's how to figure the average monthly interest expense for Months 19 through 60. First, multiply your monthly loan payment of $1,668 by 60 months, and subtract the $75,000 principal to get the total interest on the loan ($1,668 • 60 - $75,000 = $25,080). Next, subtract the $12,016 interest you will pay during the first 18 months (from your Cash Flow Projection) to get the interest during Months 19 through 60 ($25,080 - $12,016 = $13,064). Then, divide the result by 42 (the remaining months of the loan period) to get your average monthly interest expense ($13,064 ÷ 42 = $311).

Loan Principal

To get the average loan principal for Months 19 through 60, just subtract your average monthly interest of $311 from your $1,668 monthly loan payment. Your average monthly loan principal pay-back is $1,357.

Your remaining expense estimates are simple. Maintenance expenses reflect an increase as the equipment ages. Insurance expense also reflects an expected increase. Property taxes are expected to decrease each year. Talk to your local taxing authority. Your property tax liability, for this purpose, should be moved to the expense column and shown as a monthly average over the 42 month period.

Now the picture is complete! It will cost you $84,000 to build this coin laundry. You will need an additional $17,200 until your self-service laundry becomes profitable. You will not be able to withdraw any cash from the business during the first 12 months of operation, but the next 6 months will provide you with a total of $7,450 in cash ($8,050 - $600 property tax liability).

When at the end of 18 months your coin laundry reaches the projected equipment-use-factor of 20 percent, your cash withdrawal will average $1,477 per month for the next 42 months. When your loan is paid off at the end of the 60th month of operation, your monthly cash withdrawal jumps to $3,143 per month. You can now begin to appreciate the profit possibilities!

Let's see what happens to your initial investment of $26,200 at the end of five years if you maintain volume and keep costs in line. Your laundry cost $84,000 to build, but it depreciated at the rate of $715 per month. After five years, your laundry is now worth $42,900 less, or $41,100. Here's an analysis of the return on your investment (and a justification of all the work you've done!):

Depreciated Value Of Coin Laundry	—	$41,100
Cash In Bank	—	850
Cash In Coin/Bill Changer	—	500
Inventory (50% Of Monthly Purchases)	—	222
Total Cash Withdrawn In 60 Months	—	69,484
Total	—	$112,156

Over the five-year period, your $26,200 cash investment grew to $112,156. In addition to this, you now receive $3,143 per month from a business which you own free-and-clear. (You also have enjoyed some very favorable tax advantages.) With three or four of these small self-service laundries, you could have a $10,000 monthly income!

By the way, don't sell your laundry for its depreciated value. Anyone who sells a coin laundry that produces $37,716 per year for its depreciated value of $41,100 needs a mental examination!

Your Operating Plan Forecast and Cash Flow Projection are your management tools. Analyze them thoroughly before making any decisions. Your success depends on this. You can increase your cash returns by doing one or more of the following:

1. Increase revenue
2. Decrease expenses
3. Extend the life of the loan

You might reduce your cash injections considerably by doing more advertising in the first few months of operation, but don't rely on this. Success should not depend on a jack rabbit start. Your business must be adequately financed.

Before starting your business, don't neglect an analysis of your own personality. Many people are not emotionally prepared to operate on their own. They flourish with a steady job and the guidance of supervisors. Others are unwilling to take risks, and there are no rewards without risks.

A successful entrepreneur must be willing to delay gratification, to forgo the $26,200 luxury automobile now in order to "have it all" in the future. Every former employee who becomes an entrepreneur soon learns the real meaning of hard work and stress. Go for it!—but only if you're ready.

People avoid action often because they are afraid of the consequences, for action means risk and danger. Danger seems terrible from a distance: it is not so bad if you have a close look at it. And often it is a pleasant companion, adding to the zest and delight of life.

—Jawaharlal Nehru

The policy of being too cautious is the greatest risk of all.

—Jawaharlal Nehru

16

ATTENDED VERSUS UNATTENDED LAUNDRIES

THIS CHAPTER LOOKS at the pro's and con's of attended coin laundries. Some laundry owners feel that self-service laundries should be attended. Others don't. This argument has raged for as long as coin-operated laundries have existed. Make this decision for yourself, but make it before construction begins.

If your laundry is small to medium-size and you are going to have employees, they must provide additional revenue or you won't make a profit. In fact, you would have a loss, even if you were operating at your designed capacity.

ADDED REVENUE FROM EMPLOYEE SERVICES

If you have employees, your laundry can provide services to bring in additional revenue. This is the key to a successful attended coin laundry. Some of the most common services are:

- Wash-and-fold laundry service (without ironing)
- Alterations and mending
- Ironing
- Stain removal

Self-service laundries can be combined with other businesses that have employees. These employees supervise the coin laundry, and both businesses share in the cost. Dry-cleaning and convenience food markets are examples. Part-time attendants are hired to supervise the coin laundry when the other business is closed.

Your decision to have employees should not be an afterthought. The services your attendant performs must be included in your market survey and carefully analyzed. If your services are not in demand, your attendant won't generate any revenue and you won't make a profit.

ADDED COSTS FOR LEASEHOLD IMPROVEMENTS

Your attendants require additional leasehold improvements. A rest room should be added to your plan. It may even be required by law. You may also have to design your rest room to meet certain specifications for the handicapped.

Many of your leasehold improvements will depend on the services you plan to offer. You may need a sales counter. Employees need seating, as do the additional customers. Don't forget shelves for packaged clothes and clothes racks in sufficient quantities (there are never enough places to hang garments) to store clothes, sometimes for long periods of time.

You will need a separate workroom for services like mending, ironing, and stain removal. The workroom should be well lit and have plenty of extra storage space. The doors should have locks. When chemicals are used (for stain removal), the workroom must have forced air ventilation.

Attended versus Unattended Laundries

ADDED COSTS FOR EQUIPMENT

An attended coin laundry requires additional equipment. The type of equipment will depend on the services you plan to offer. The equipment might include:

- Cash register
- Scale for weighing clothes
- Calculator
- Telephone
- Wrapping paper dispenser
- Tape dispenser
- Clothes bagging stand
- Bins or baskets for clothes
- Iron
- Sewing machine

If you expect to have a high-volume self-service laundry and also do a high-volume wash-and-fold business at the same time, you will need additional large capacity washers and dryers. These machines should be located behind the sales counter or in the workroom, away from the coin laundry customers. To prevent mistakes, plan your laundry so that your attendants can tag, sort and fold clothes away from self-service customers.

Don't make your attendants compete with your self-service customers for the washers, dryers, and clothes-folding tables. This angers customers and promotes clothes theft, lost clothes, mixed up orders, and confusion when your laundry is busy. It also reduces equipment cycles, particularly during high-volume times, such as on weekends. When you lose cycles, you lose revenue.

ADDED OPERATING EXPENSES

You have a number of additional expenses when you have an attended coin laundry. You need additional space and this means additional rent expense. The amount of extra space depends on the type of services you offer. It also depends on the volume of business you expect from each service.

You have additional accounting expenses to maintain payroll records and to file quarterly and annual payroll tax reports. You may even need to file reports with county and/or local government.

You need a telephone and you will need to advertise your services. You need to purchase office supplies and operating supplies such as: hangers, tape, wrapping paper, laundry additives, clothes bags, chemicals, toilet paper, hand soap, etc. The type and amount of these expenses depend on the services you offer.

PAYROLL EXPENSES

Your largest additional operating expense is your payroll. Besides an hourly wage, as an employer you are required to pay payroll taxes based on the dollar amount of your payroll. Contact Federal, state and local taxing authorities to get a package of tax instructions, pamphlets and forms called the "Employer's Tax Package." For your Federal tax package, contact the nearest offices of the Internal Revenue Service and Social Security Administration.

Your state requires you to pay unemployment insurance and accident insurance when you have employees. Business license fees are often based on the dollar amount of your payroll or the number of people you employ. Check carefully! Your state, county, and local governments may also have other taxes in store for you when you become an employer.

Use this checklist when estimating payroll taxes for your Operating Plan Forecast and Cash Flow Projection:

1. Federal Social Security Tax
2. Federal Unemployment Tax

Attended versus Unattended Laundries

3. State Unemployment Insurance
4. Worker's Compensation Insurance
5. Business License
6. Miscellaneous Local Taxes

If you are an employer, you become a collector for the government. You are required to withhold taxes from your employees' wages and make periodic payments to the taxing authorities. Contact Federal, state and local taxing authorities for this information. The following list is provided as a guide:

1. Employee's Federal Social Security Tax
2. Employee's Federal Income Taxes
3. Employee's State Income Taxes
4. Employee's State Unemployment Insurance
5. Workers' Compensation Insurance (Employee's Contribution)
6. Miscellaneous Taxes

CAUTION: Tax laws vary considerably from area to area. Laws are constantly being added or amended at the Federal, state, county, and city levels. They may even vary from zone to zone within a city. These lists may not cover all required taxes. Make sure you contact all the taxing authorities that have jurisdiction over your location.

You can get a copy of the Federal Minimum Wage and Hour Laws from the local office of the U. S. Department of Labor. Among other things, these laws specify limits on employee age, wages, and hours worked. Study these laws carefully. There are substantial penalties for violations. Most states have laws governing employer-employee relationships. Your state's Department of Labor will give you a copy of these laws.

If you have never been an employer, this probably sounds complicated. It all becomes fairly routine, however, once you work with it. Your accountant can set up your system for you. If you do it yourself, the taxing authorities can answer questions as they arise. (See Chapter 21 for more information on accounting procedures.)

The important thing to remember when figuring employee costs is that you pay a number of taxes in addition to wages. These taxes can be 12 percent (or more) of the hourly wage, depending on the location of your business. The minimum cost to have your coin laundry attended full time would be about $2,000 per month. *This is just for one employee per shift!*

ATTENDANTS — THE ADVANTAGES

Why have employees? The main reason is to make more profit with a small amount of additional investment in leasehold improvements and equipment. The key to that profit is a strong demand for your services, skillful employee management, and meticulous control of your operating expenses.

There are other advantages. Many laundry owners feel that an attended coin laundry draws more customers than an unattended one. Some customers feel more secure if the self-service laundry has an attendant. There is less opportunity for vandals and thieves to ply their trade.

ATTENDANTS — THE DISADVANTAGES

You are offering a position with low income, few (if any) benefits, and little chance for advancement. This means that you will attract employees with limited skills and little motivation. Expect employee turnover to be high. You will be running a continuous training program. The result will be frequent errors, many of them costly.

You will be addressing a number of employee-related problems, including illness, absenteeism, emotional fluctuations, and poorly maintained time schedules. You cannot rely on your employees to run your business, so there will be a need for constant supervision.

Attended versus Unattended Laundries

You must constantly be on guard against employee theft, one of the biggest problems facing small business in America today. Employee theft is responsible for a substantial number of business failures. It doesn't take much to destroy a new business.

When you add employees, you increase your legal exposure. Laundry owners have been sued by customers for a variety of reasons. Laundry attendants have insulted customers, destroyed or stolen their property, and even assaulted them. Employees have also filed lawsuits against employers for a variety of reasons, real or imagined. These suits are costly to a coin laundry owner, no matter who wins.

Employees often develop attitude problems, presenting a serious obstacle to good customer relations. Your employees need constant supervision if you are to maintain good customer relations. Never forget that a clean, well-managed unattended laundry will outperform a poorly managed one that is <u>attended</u>.

AN ALTERNATIVE

It's possible to increase your revenue and have your laundry supervised without hiring a single employee. Consider subleasing part of your space to another entrepreneur whose business requires very little space. This person can operate a business from the subleased space with a relatively small investment.

The types of businesses that could be conducted from a subleased space are limited only by the imagination. You would be wise, however, to choose one that will attract additional laundry customers. A money order and check cashing service would be a good choice. Some laundry owners sublease their wash-and-fold service. Others, their mending and ironing.

Two things you must consider before you sublease part of your space: First, make sure that your lease does not prohibit you from subleasing. Second, there are strict legal definitions as to what constitutes an employee. Ask your attorney.

The provisions of the sublease are just as critical to your success as your main lease. A bad sublessee can destroy your business if it's too weak to protect you. Consult your attorney and ask for help in preparing your sublease.

Many department stores and mass merchandisers sublet space within their stores. Their attorneys develop strong leases that protect them from abuses by lessees. Obtain and review as many of these leases as possible before developing your own. It's a free education that might prevent future problems.

Your success will not depend on whether your laundry is attended or unattended or whether or not part of your space is subleased by another business. It does depend on your ability to make good business decisions. You cannot make good business decisions unless you have the necessary accurate facts.

Conduct a detailed market survey on all businesses you plan to operate from your location. Estimate revenues and determine the expenses of each. Develop an Operating Plan Forecast and Cash Flow Projection based on this information. If you don't, you are courting failure. Why take that chance?

17

GETTING
FINANCED

IF YOU DON"T HAVE the proper attitude about money, getting financing for your business can be a nightmare instead of a challenge. Money is only a tool. It's just another item to be purchased for your new coin laundry.

Many people select a business based on the amount of money they think they can borrow. This kind of thinking limits success. Money is no different from equipment or leasehold improvements. It's purchased the same way, by getting bids and buying the best deal available in the marketplace.

FINANCIAL SOURCES

Money is plentiful. You have more sources for money than you have for washers and dryers. Three main sources for financing are: private sources, leasing companies, and lending institutions.

Private Sources

Those who purchase money from a private source generally get it from family members or close friends. Other sources are a partner or a group of private investors. Private sources usually demand more control than leasing companies or lending institutions.

Leasing Companies

Leasing companies buy the equipment and then lease it to the laundry owner. Normally the equipment is leased at a fixed rate for a predetermined amount of time, such as five years. At the end of the contract, the laundry owner is usually able to purchase the leased equipment at a predetermined price.

Leasing is generally the most expensive way to finance a new coin laundry, but there are advantages. Leasing companies are usually more flexible than banks. They are normally willing to tailor a program to fit your needs. In this age of variable rate loans, you can often lease your equipment at a fixed rate. There are also tax advantages from leasing. Check with your accountant before deciding.

Leasing companies sometimes lease more than just equipment. Some lease programs include all the coin laundry construction. Some have even been known to include the utility hookup fees. There are some equipment manufacturers and distributors that have their own lease programs. Look in the *Yellow Pages* for the names of leasing companies.

Lending Institutions

Most small businesses buy their money from commercial lending institutions. These include banks, savings and loan companies, and financial service companies. In most cases, this money is less expensive so you are able to make a greater profit. Prices for money vary considerably among banks. Be sure to compare prices and lending terms before making any decisions.

Getting Financed

BEGIN EARLY

Many experienced business people start lining up potential sources even before they select their location. By that time, you should have a list of potential sources for financing. You should have met with each one on your list at least once.

Typical loans for coin laundries fall in the range of $50,000 to $150,000. Banks classify loans of this size as "small loans," and some banks are not interested in making small loans to new businesses. Make sure you eliminate these banks from your list during your first call so that you are not wasting your time.

ESTABLISH A RELATIONSHIP

Imagine that you are a bank loan officer. How would you treat someone who walked in unannounced and asked for a loan for some vague business idea without presenting a written plan? This is not the way to arrange financing. When meeting with bank loan officers, always try to see things from their viewpoint.

It takes as much effort to arrange satisfactory financing as it does to find your business location, do your market survey, negotiate your lease, build your coin laundry, and purchase your equipment. In fact, all of these steps are required if you expect to get the best financing deal available in the marketplace. Prepare for every meeting. Never walk into a bank and ask to see a loan officer unless you have an appointment.

Briefly state the purpose of your initial visit. Inform the loan officer that you may be shopping for money sometime within the next 12 months. You want to determine if his or her bank makes small loans to small businesses in the range of $50,000 to $150,000. If not, don't waste the loan officer's time or yours.

If the bank makes these loans, what next? Inform the loan officer that it's too early to go into detail. You face several months of hard work before you will have a business plan. If you proceed with the business, you will present a complete plan, including a financial statement. In the meantime, you want to meet with the loan officer occasionally to discuss your progress. Let the loan officer know that suggestions will be valuable to you.

It's important to develop a good long-term business relationship with your banker. This cannot be accomplished unless both parties are totally honest. Have periodic meetings during your planning stage. Let your banker share in the development of your business. It's harder for lending institutions to turn down financing for businesses they help plan.

WHAT WILL THE BANKER WANT TO KNOW?

The lending institution will look at two things before lending money—you, and your proposal. They want to know if you have the necessary knowledge and experience to succeed in your proposed business. Make them aware of any training or help you may have received from manufacturers, distributors, business seminars, consultants, or books. They will want to know your personal history. They look for character traits like stability and honesty, and a good credit rating.

They will examine your personal financial statement to determine if you have collateral to secure the loan. Collateral can be a home, vehicles, or other items of value. Don't try to predict their evaluation of your financial condition. A person with $100,000 cash and no real estate may find it more difficult to borrow money than a home owner with only a small amount of cash.

THE PROPOSAL

Type your formal proposal and put it into an attractive binder. Include your personal resume, your business plan, and your request for financing.

Personal Resume

Will the loan be repaid?—on time? This is the main concern of every loan officer. Your personal resume should make your banker confident that you will do just that. Now it's time to brag. Don't be afraid to toot your horn, but make sure that you do it truthfully. Develop your resume around the following points:

- Personal history
- Education
- Work history
- Character traits
- Credit references
- Achievements
- Personal references
- Financial Statement

Your resume should show how your knowledge and experience will contribute to a successful self-service laundry business. It makes little difference whether you are a janitor, a manager, an accountant, a mechanic, a construction worker, or a salesman. All this talent is required to build and operate a successful coin laundry. Think about that!

Business Plan

The main thrust of your proposal will be on the business. Your plan should include everything that you have accomplished in preparation for the construction of your laundry. Include the following in your proposal:

- Why you selected the coin laundry business
- Pictures of modern self-service laundries
- Why you selected the location
- Your market survey
- Your analysis of the market survey
- A justification of your revenue projections
- How you determined the size of the store
- How you selected your equipment
- A drawing of the store layout
- The logic supporting your layout

- A copy of the proposed lease
- The lease amendments you negotiated
- The estimated construction and equipment costs
- Your advertising program
- Your Operating Plan Forecast
- Your Cash Flow Projection
- Your request for a loan

You will find it easy to write your business plan if you use the same step-by-step procedures that were used in Chapter 15. Be prepared to answer questions and to justify your figures.

Request For Financing

Be specific in your request for a loan. Tell the loan officer exactly how much money you want and how it will be used. Your request should state the interest rate you desire and the number of months you require to pay back the principal. Don't be afraid to haggle on the points. It shows good business sense to try to get a low interest rate.

It's better to request too much money than not enough. Asking for too much money can be justified as taking a conservative approach. Not asking for enough money is a danger signal to the loan officer. It hints that you don't know what you're doing.

THE PRESENTATION

Your formal proposal is complete, and you have several typed copies in attractive binders. You are ready to make your presentations. You have met with a number of different lending institutions and selected two or three of the best possibilities. Start making appointments with these lending institutions.

Arrange to meet with the loan officer and other bank officers who may be involved in the loan decision. Allow enough time to present your proposal and answer questions. Hold your meeting in a private room (most banks have conference rooms). Ask that there be no telephone calls or other interruptions. Present a copy of your proposal to each person at the meeting.

Be confident when making your proposal. If you've used the guidelines in this book, your proposal will be as good as any they have seen. Encourage questions. If you can't answer one, make a note to get back to them later. Don't guess! If you have followed this book, your business plan will withstand the toughest examination. In fact, it already has—yours!

WHAT IF YOU ARE TURNED DOWN ???

If for some reason your request for financing is denied, find out why. Usually it's for one of the following reasons:

1. Their asset-to-loan ratio is temporarily out of balance, according to legal guidelines. (Not your fault.)
2. Because of limited funds, they are making loans only to their most solid customers, their large depositors. (Also not your fault.)
3. They don't feel that you are prepared to assume the responsibility.
4. The project is not feasible.
5. You failed to communicate.

Make the necessary corrections (if any are required), and present your proposal to other lending institutions. Do this until you are successful. The hard work is already done, so why not present your proposal 50 more times if you have to. Persistence usually pays off for those who don't quit. If you still can't get adequate financing, try alternate sources.

One is the Small Business Administration. The SBA will sometimes make small business loans directly to entrepreneurs if they have been turned down by at least two banks. Keep fighting until you win. It's good practice for the main event—the construction and operation of your business.

Coin Laundries — Road to Financial Security

People are compelled to classify everything. Adam and Eve classified themselves as "man" and "woman." After they had children it became "us" and "them." Our society seems to have an infinite number of classifications. If we're not classified by religion or nationalities, we're classified like crayons—black, yellow, red, brown, white, etc.

These classifications are sometimes called "minorities." Minorities can be race, religion, nationality, or sex. Go to the Small Business Administration if you are a minority, or even if you're not. Ask what Government programs are available to you. If there is a program that fits your needs, accept it. That's good business and that's what this book is all about.

18

SECURITY

THE SOARING CRIME rate has made small business focus a considerable amount of attention on security. No business is immune to crime. Almost every business will experience it in some form or another during its operations.

The basic problems are robbery, theft and vandalism. Retail firms also face schemes invented by con men to swindle profits. Quick-change artists bilk money from busy clerks, and counterfeit money is circulated. Foreign coin is used in the vast numbers of vending machines throughout the country.

Problems are not always caused by nameless, faceless criminals, but by insiders. One retailer installed computerized automatic change making equipment after receiving complaints from customers about being shortchanged. Over 80 percent of his cash register clerks quit, and profits increased considerably. His employees had been doing more than shortchanging customers.

EMPLOYEE THEFT

If you are an employer, you may become the victim of an employee. If this sounds too harsh or cynical, attend some seminars on small business for a quick dose of reality. Employee theft is a very serious problem! It has bankrupted many small businesses. What makes this problem so complex is that employee theft is difficult to detect and even harder to prove.

Numerous laws protect the employees, but little consideration is given to the employer. Only a small percentage of employee thefts result in a conviction. Even if there is a conviction, there is little chance that the employer will recover the loss.

If an employer sues an employee for damages and loses, the thief often sues the employer—and wins. Prosecution is not worth the risk and thieves know it. It's one reason why there is so much employee theft.

Employee theft often goes undetected for long periods of time. By the time it is detected, it's usually out of control. Employers generally like their employees, and it's human nature to trust those you like. Being loyal to an employee, however, doesn't guarantee loyalty in return.

It's important to understand the impact that employee theft can have on your business. Consider the theft of five cases of pop, two cartons of candy, and a few boxes of laundry detergent. Many people would consider this insignificant. Unfortunately, so do many judges. The dollar value might be less than 1 percent of your gross revenue, but it could easily be 20 percent of your monthly cash withdrawal. It doesn't take much of this to destroy your new business before you have a chance to make it successful.

The following are forms of employee theft that often can occur in attended coin laundries:

- Theft of supplies
- Theft of inventory
- Shortchanging customers
- Unreported sales of services

Security

- Theft of money from coin boxes
- Theft of money from the cash register
- Theft of equipment, tools, furnishings, etc.
- Unreported ("back door") sales of inventory
- Theft of customers' clothes or other possessions.
- Theft of owner's or other employees' personal items

Hold All Keys

Most coin operated machines have separate access to the controls and coin boxes. Each has its own lock. Laundry owners usually provide employees with keys to the access doors, but not to the coin boxes. By having access to the controls, employees can manually operate a machine if it fails to start when the customer inserts coins.

Separate locks prevent theft, right? Wrong! Employees have been known to open the access panels of washers and dryers, start the machines for customers, then keep the money. This type of theft is almost impossible to detect unless the machines are equipped with a cycle counter.

Employees have used access panel keys to steal products from vending machines. Others have sold products by placing signs on the machines stating "Out of Order—See Attendant." Enterprising attendants have even fashioned cardboard diversion slides to bypass the coin box so they can collect the coin by opening the access panels.

Reduce your chances of being victimized. Don't give access panel keys to your attendants. Instead, tell them to have the customer fill out a refund slip if a machine malfunctions. Mail the refund directly to the customer. This also reduces cheating by your customers. Keep track of the refunds and learn which customers are repeatedly filing false claims.

Screen Job Applicants

Carefully screen all applicants, checking as many previous employment references as possible. Don't rely on one or two references because they can be misleading. Employers sometimes conceal facts for fear of being sued by a former employee.

In the past, some employers required lie detector tests as a condition of employment. Recent Federal legislation has made this practice illegal in the private sector. Only Federal, state and local governments can use this tool.

Schedule Frequent and Unexpected Visits

Your best defense against theft is vigilance. Vary the times that you visit your laundry. Frequent and unexpected visits can prevent your employees from selling services and keeping the money. Check the written sales tickets against the services that are being performed. Make sure that payment was received when you total the receipts at the end of the day.

Unexpected visits keep employees alert. During each visit, point out work that needs to be done. Follow up on their progress during your next surprise visit. Your laundry will be cleaner and better attended. You can prevent a lot of problems by properly managing your employees. Busy employees don't have time to get into mischief.

Run Frequent Audits

Audits are a management tool that is often neglected. Audit everything—your money, operating supplies, office supplies, tools, equipment, and product inventory. Besides being a deterrent to theft, audits prevent waste. Frequent audits will help control your expenses.

Control Your Inventory

Keep inventories of office supplies, operating supplies and products in a locked room. Don't give the key to your employees. You stock the vending machines. You dispense supplies as they are needed. Some laundry owners feel that this much control is a nuisance, but most agree it's effective in reducing theft.

Security

Summary

You can't prevent employee theft, but good management slows it down. Don't give keys to your employees. Screen all job applicants carefully. Visit your coin laundry frequently and unexpectedly. Run periodic audits on money, supplies, tools, and inventory. Maintain tight inventory control. Do all of these things, and you will hold your losses to a minimum.

ROBBERY, THEFT, AND VANDALISM

Crime is out of control in this country. It's no longer a "city problem." Drugs have brought robbery and theft to every community. Almost every retailer has experienced some form of criminal activity. Even alarm companies have been broken into and burglarized. Careful planning and good management can help reduce the number of incidents in your self-service laundry.

Maintain Good Volume

The best deterrent to robbery, theft and vandalism is people. Self-service laundries with lots of customers experience fewer incidents than stores with low business volume. You are more likely to have problems late at night when customer traffic is light. Set an early closing time. A few extra quarters from late night business aren't worth the added risk of staying open late.

Avoid Patterns

You are at risk when you handle large amounts of money on a regular basis. A robber doesn't have to be a mental giant to realize that you haul your money from the laundry to the bank—periodically. It's easy to conceal $1,200 in large bills, but how do you conceal 4,800 quarters? Anyone but a weight lifter will have the telltale signs of a red face and a canted gait when leaving the coin laundry with a large bag of coins.

Vary your collection time, and vary the time that you take the money from your store. Count money in private, away from the store whenever possible. Be alert for anyone observing or follow-

223

ing you. Avoid bank deposit boxes, which are especially dangerous.

To discourage burglars, some laundry owners remove all money from the laundry daily and leave the empty cash boxes in plain sight when the laundry is closed. While this may discourage burglars, it encourages robbers who know that money is taken to the store in the morning and from the store at night—every day.

Maintain Good Visibility

Visibility is a good deterrent to robbery, theft, and vandalism. You will have fewer problems if your store has lots of windows and is well lit. Locate your coin/bill changer in a high visibility area. Make sure the police or the security patrol can see it from outside the store.

Purchase Good Locks

Good locks are important, whether the coin laundry is attended or not. A skilful thief can pick dozens of tube locks and steal your money while doing his own laundry. Thieves have become very sophisticated. Some travel the States in motor homes containing computerized lock information and state-of-the-art key-making equipment.

Choose your locks carefully. Many people have keys that fit standard locks on coin-operated equipment. These people include former or current employees of equipment manufacturers and distributors, lock manufacturers and distributors, locksmiths, route operators, service companies, etc.

SLUGS AND FOREIGN COIN

Slugs and foreign coin have always been a problem for coin laundry owners. Coin slide manufacturers and coin laundry equipment manufacturers are working to develop new products to eliminate this problem. Nothing is guaranteed to be 100 percent effective, but you can reduce your risk. Purchase good slides that can be adjusted to reject a high percentage of slugs and foreign coin.

The advent of magnetic ticket-operated machines by one manufacturer has helped eliminate this problem when tickets are sold over the counter. But if tickets are purchased from coin-operated ticket-dispensing machines, slugs and foreign coin can still be a problem. More research is needed before this problem is solved.

SECURITY SYSTEMS

Because of big increases in criminal activity, the security industry is one of the fastest growing industries. Changes are taking place almost daily, and new equipment is continually appearing. Take the time to become familiar with this equipment before deciding on a security plan for your new laundry.

Mirror Windows

In the past few years, retail stores have started using mirror windows to reduce theft. Since most people recognize them, they can be an inexpensive deterrent to robbery, theft, and vandalism. Without breaking the mirror, a potential troublemaker cannot be sure if a person is watching or if a camera is monitoring their moves. The mirror can be wired into an alarm system by attaching a glass-breakage module.

Some municipalities have laws that govern this type of surveillance. Thoroughly investigate the law before installing mirror windows.

Alarm Systems

Because of rising crime rates, burglar alarm companies have sprung up like weeds. Although not foolproof, an alarm system can reduce your vulnerability to burglary, theft, and vandalism. These systems range from a few hundred to several thousand dollars. Compare different systems before making a choice, including checking your library for copies of *Consumer Reports* magazines that evaluate alarm systems.

Be Careful. It's easy to pay too much money for an alarm system. For about $600 (plus your own labor), you can install a simple system that includes the console, door sensors, glass breakage sensors, motion detectors, and a dialer. The dialer can be programmed to dial either your home or a central monitoring station.

It's not unusual to pay from $2,500 to $3,500 to a commercial alarm company for the same amount of protection. Their prices usually include installation, but there is still a lot of fat in their pricing. Be sure to dicker hard before signing a purchase agreement.

Burglar alarms are heavily regulated in some areas. Check local laws before ordering an alarm system.

Closed Circuit Television

For unattended laundries, which are vulnerable to theft and vandalism, closed circuit television systems can be used as a deterrent. They can also help identify criminals. These systems range in price from a few hundred to several thousand dollars, depending on their complexity. Even the most elaborate system is inexpensive compared to the cost of an employee.

Exposed cameras are protected by security cages. Their presence tends to deter most vandalism. By using a time lapse system, the recorder can tape for many hours on a standard video cassette. The cassettes can be played on any home video recorder. Some systems even indicate the time of day on the recording.

The addition of a monitor (television set) to the system will allow someone in the vicinity to watch the store. It's possible to make arrangements with nearby retail businesses (or even private homes) to monitor store activity for a small fee. Cable is required to connect the camera to the monitor, and this does limit the distance for remote monitoring.

Security

Your local police department is a good source of information. They can help you determine which kind of security measures are best for your laundry. Before buying a system, ask the distributor for the names of current users. Talk to them before making a purchase.

The real significance of crime is in its being a breach of faith with the community of mankind.

—Joseph Conrad

Why the injustice and the cruelty go on—year after year—century after century—without change—because—as they grow older—people become—tolerant!

—Samuel Nathaniel Behrman

No program of crime prevention will be effective without a massive overhaul of the lower criminal courts.

—National Crime Commission

19

ADVERTISING
AND PROMOTION

E NTREPRENEURS WASTE MILLIONS of advertising
dollars every year. They are constantly plagued by high-
pressure salespeople armed with statistics showing their advertising program is the best. As a result, most entrepreneurs end up
spending too much money for too little return.

Analyze and compare each advertising program before spending your money. You must be able to answer these questions if you
want results:

1. Who are my prospective customers?
2. What advertising media reaches them?
3. How often will they be exposed to my message?
4. What is the cost per thousand prospects who receive my
   message?

229

Coin Laundries — Road to Financial Independence

Don't rely on advertising media salespeople for the answers. They have their own interests at heart. Instead, use your market survey to answer the first two questions. Answers to the third question will come from your best judgment. The answer to the fourth question is a matter of simple arithmetic.

If your market survey doesn't provide answers to the first two questions, conduct a survey that does. Otherwise you will spend advertising dollars based on conjecture instead of facts.

Look at this comparison of two different advertising programs that you might use:

Media	Radio–10 Spots	Direct Mail To A Selected Prospect List Of 5,000 Names
Total Cost	$150	$2,000
Total Homes Reached	20,000	5,000
Estimated Number Of Homes Reached In The Practical Marketing Area Of The Store	200	5,000
Estimated Number Of Prospects Exposed To Message	20	3,000
Cost To Reach 1,000 Prospects	$7,500	$667

Radio covers a large area, but most listeners will be outside your market. You must estimate the number of households in your market that will receive your message. Check the library for market statistics on local radio stations. This will help you make an accurate estimate.

Just because a radio is turned on doesn't mean that a prospect is listening. Radio listeners can be teens or even pre-teens. They are certainly not self-service laundry prospects. Others in the home may be talking on the telephone, sleeping, or doing something else while the radio is on, and will not hear your message. Estimate the number of prospects that will actually receive your message.

Your local "rock" station could reach 20,000 households between 6 and 7 p.m., but only reach 200 in your market. What if the listeners in 120 of these households are children? If prospective customers failed to hear your message in another 60 households, it would only reach 20 prospects.

On the other hand, if 40 percent of the direct mail prospects throw away your letter without opening it, your cost per thousand prospects for the direct mail program is $667. Compare this to $7,500 for radio advertising.

The objective of advertising is not to "tickle" prospects, it's to make them customers. Your radio message may reach 20 prospects, but how many of these will become customers? You will soon learn to estimate this by watching for new faces and an increase in sales after running an advertising program.

The bottom line is how many advertising dollars will it cost you to get a new customer? If 10 percent of radio-listening prospects become customers, the radio spots would produce 2 customers at a cost of $75.00 each. The direct mail program would produce 300 customers at a cost of $6.67 each.

The previous example should not influence your advertising media decisions because every market is different. Each will require a complete analysis. Just because a program works (or didn't) in one area, doesn't necessarily mean that you will get the same results in another.

Remember this! Make absolutely sure of your facts and figures when making an advertising program analysis. Check all statements and figures, especially when provided by advertising media salespeople. Use your library. It's a good source for information on your local newspapers, radio, and television stations.

TELEVISION, RADIO, NEWSPAPER ADVERTISING

The market for a self-service coin laundry is usually a small geographical area. This is particularly true in metropolitan areas. In heavily populated areas, television, radio, and major newspapers are usually too expensive, unless you own a chain of self-service laundries.

There is a way to reduce the cost of television, radio, and newspaper advertising. Try forming an association with other self-service laundry owners to share in advertising expenses. This is done by tagging the names and locations of several different laundries at the end of each ad. The cost is then divided among the participants.

Radio advertising can be very effective in rural markets where there are only a few stations. Many times the format of a particular station is directed toward local listeners because it features local news, local current events, job offers, and items for resale. Rural market advertising rates are usually very reasonable.

Use the "rifle" approach rather than the "shotgun" approach in advertising, particularly if your laundry is located in a metropolitan area. In other words, concentrate your effort within your market. Don't blanket the entire city with television or newspaper ads, hoping to reach some of your prospects.

DIRECT MAIL ADVERTISING

Direct mail and door hangers are two examples of the "rifle" approach. Door hangers are plastic bags that contain advertising from several merchants. The bags are hung on doors by delivery people. You only pay for your advertising message to go to the areas you designate. Companies who perform this service can be found under "Advertising—Direct Mail" in the *Yellow Pages*.

Advertising and Promotion

One of the most effective ways to promote a coin-operated laundry is the 3½-inch by 5½-inch postcard. Have a printer produce cards with a "free wash" coupon and your advertising message. Mail or hand deliver them to your list of self-service laundry prospects from your market survey.

The Maytag Company manufactures ticket-operated washers and dryers in addition to their coin-operated laundry equipment. They offer sixteen different plastic tickets with printed circuits. The tickets come in boxes of 1,000 tickets. You can specify a particular ticket, and then set your machines so that they will only accept that ticket.

These tickets can be attached to the postcards offering a free wash or dry. This works particularly well in unattended coin laundries where there is no attendant to start the machines for a customer with a free wash coupon. Hand delivering the cards can save a lot of money in postage. (It may also improve your physical condition.)

SPECIALTY NEWSPAPERS

Local newspaper weekly inserts (sometimes known as "shoppers") can be effective. They contain bargains from local merchants, and they are widely read. They are also relatively inexpensive.

Another effective (and inexpensive) means of carrying your message are "coupon shoppers." These are strictly advertising papers, normally published monthly. The papers contain coupons that are clipped by the reader and presented to the merchant for savings on a product or service.

YELLOW PAGES

Yellow Pages advertising carries your message to prospective customers who move into your market. Be sure to list all the services you offer. This advertising is particularly effective in markets that attract a large number of tourists who are usually unfamiliar with the area. The size of the ad is not nearly as important as its content.

SIGNS AND DISPLAYS

Scheduled promotions are not the only means of promoting your laundry. A large, well-lit exterior sign will advertise your laundry and its services to passersby. Your message is displayed 24 hours a day, 365 days a year.

Good window signs and displays are effective. Make sure they are easily seen by prospective customers who walk by your store. Don't forget to use attractive indoor signs and displays to promote your services.

A DEVIOUS PROMOTION

Some laundry owners record license plate numbers on automobiles parked in front of competitive coin laundries. Names and addresses are then obtained from the state records division., and postcards containing free wash coupons (or tickets) are mailed out.

Be on the alert for competitors who may be using this tactic against you. Counteraction should be swift, effective, and legal. If a cordial meeting with your competitor fails to produce positive results, some other course of action may be called for. You can always do the same to your competitor, but that may not solve the problem.

Consider hiring a 275 pound weight lifter who is trained in self defense. Position him on the public sidewalk in front of your competitor's laundry, and have him hand out free wash coupons for use at your laundry. This should result in an agreement to discontinue the nonsense and return to more ethical promotions.

Do not take any retaliatory action that is not legal. Check with your attorney.

No matter what media is selected to convey your message, effective advertising for a coin laundry must:

Advertising and Promotion

- Be properly timed
- Offer a "Deal"
- Have continuity

PROPER TIMING

Before you can fully understand the importance of timing, you must first understand your customers. We are a nation of spenders—not savers. Your customers' money is often spent before they receive it. Many people spend money so fast they don't even have a bank account. Their weekly paychecks buy several money orders to pay bills, and the balance is gone within hours!

There is a lot of competition for these dollars. This includes landlords, utilities, other coin laundries and retailers who sell food, clothing, automobiles, recreation, etc. You either get there first, or you lose the business. Your customer will launder clothes at the home of a friend or parent, or even in the bathtub when short of cash. This is business that is lost forever.

Schedule your advertising around paydays or the dates of welfare and social security payments. Paid holidays offer a chance to increase your business because clothes are usually laundered before and after a holiday. Sometimes a holiday will coincide with a particularly large pay period (such as month end), and business will boom.

There is always heavy retail advertising around paid holidays. This tends to create a lot of retail activity in the market and increased competition for the dollar. Get your message out before the dollars are gone! The one exception is the period around Christmas and New Year's when the coin laundry business is generally slow. The dollars go for presents.

OFFER A DEAL

The most effective type of advertising is "promotional." Promotional advertising promises the customer some kind of a deal and gives an incentive to break a habit and go to an unfamiliar coin laundry. Here are some typical deals:

- Free wash or dry
- Reduced prices for washing and drying
- Free or reduced prices on services
- Discounts on soap or soft drinks
- Coupons for free merchandise at other retail stores

The deal doesn't have to be reduced prices or free merchandise. Hire entertainment for your promotional events. Bands, clowns, magicians, pony rides and carnival rides, can all be employed to attract new customers.

One laundry owner hired a belly dancer and promoted Thursday nights as "men's night." The promotion worked <u>too</u> well. It was discontinued when it brought masses of people from all over town who jammed the parking lot and coin laundry and disrupted the entire shopping center.

Did someone say that coin laundries were dull? Promotional ideas are limited only by the imagination!

CONTINUITY ADVERTISING

For maximum effect, promotions should be scheduled to run on a continuous basis. This can be bimonthly, monthly, or at the very least, every other month. Many in the advertising industry claim it takes an average of three exposures to an advertising message before communication is achieved. If the delay between messages is too long, momentum is lost and advertising dollars are wasted.

Another reason for continuity of advertising is to maintain your customer base. Coin laundry customers tend to be highly mobile. A coin laundry can lose 25 percent of its customers in a year. If you don't advertise on a regular basis, your volume will most likely decline.

Advertising and Promotion

STARTING YOUR NEW LAUNDRY

The first few months of a new business are critical. It's a time when you cannot afford to experiment. Mistakes can result in disaster. Carefully plan your advertising program well in advance of your opening date. Place orders for any advertising materials you may need, and make sure they are delivered long before they are needed.

If you are running television, radio, newspaper, or direct mail advertising, schedule your ads far in advance. Do not leave everything for the last minute or it won't get done. You are going to be very busy the minute that your coin laundry opens.

YOUR BEST BET

The following promotional program is the most reliable for opening a new self-service laundry:

1. Conduct a market survey and compile a large list of prospective customer names and addresses—the more the better.
2. Mail, hire the delivery of, or personally deliver free wash coupons (or tickets) to your list of prospective customers. Do this at least three times during the first 60 days of business.
3. Run a 25¢-wash and 25¢-dry program until volume is established. Advertise this program in your prospective customer mailing and by ample use of window signs and banners.
4. Create a carnival atmosphere in and around your coin laundry. Use flags, banners, signs, and helium-filled balloons.

After your coin laundry is established, try other promotional programs. That is part of the enjoyment and challenge of running your own business. There is great satisfaction in seeing your ideas result in increased business—and increased profits.

At the conclusion of each promotional program, evaluate it:

- How much did my volume increase?
- What did it cost me to get this increase?
- What is the long-term effect (momentum) of the promotion?

As your business grows, don't forget what made you successful. Keep doing the basics.

Doing business without advertising is like winking at a girl in the dark. You know what you are doing, but nobody else does.

—Stewart Henderson Britt

20

MAINTAINING
AND REPAIRING
YOUR EQUIPMENT

YOUR COIN LAUNDRY equipment will need regular maintenance. Even new equipment malfunctions and needs repair. Don't be concerned. With proper instruction you can learn to maintain and repair your equipment without too much difficulty.

A factory service instructor once said it was easier to train a novice than to instruct an experienced know-it-all. He proved his point at the end of his two-week service seminar. A 22-year-old home economist solved tough hands-on repair problems while an appliance serviceman with years of experience managed to fail.

ATTEND SERVICE SEMINARS

Hiring a service firm to maintain and repair your equipment is not only expensive, it's usually unnecessary. Most equipment manufacturers conduct periodic service seminars which are only a few days long. They are held at the factory or at different locations throughout the country.

Some factory service seminars are free and some are not. The cost (if any) is small when compared to hiring outside help to repair your equipment. Be sure to get a schedule of factory service seminars from each manufacturer. Attend as many as possible. You'll be glad you did.

ORGANIZE YOUR SERVICE INFORMATION

Have the following information available for every piece of equipment:

- Installation instructions
- Maintenance manual
- Parts manual
- Wiring diagram
- Maintenance calendar

When organized properly, this information provides quick answers to most repair problems.

Plot the maintenance requirements for your equipment on a calendar and review it weekly. Proper maintenance extends the life of your equipment and prevents many costly repairs.

THE QUICK-REFERENCE ADDRESS BOOK

Another valuable aid is a quick-reference address book that contains the names, addresses, and telephone numbers of the following:

1. Equipment manufacturers and distributors
2. Their service technicians
3. Parts distributors
4. Nearest emergency technical help

Maintaining and Repairing Your Equipment

Make sure you have the names of personnel on the parts order desks. List their telephone numbers if different from the corporate headquarters. When a company is located in another time zone, record this and the business hours beside the address.

You can save money by calling toll-free numbers. Dial 1-800-555-1212 and ask the operator if the company has one. For a nominal charge you can order a toll-free directory from American Telephone and Telegraph Company. (Call 1-800-426-8686.)

REPAIR PARTS

Keep an inventory of parts with a high failure rate. Local parts suppliers never seem to carry a sufficient inventory. Sometimes a machine will set idle for weeks while you wait for a critical part. When the part finally arrives—Guess what? They shipped the wrong one!

Much "down time" can be eliminated if you take time to gather and record specific information before faced with a crisis. Maintain a list of parts sources for each piece of equipment. List the minimum order charges and volume discounts from each source. A fifty-dollar minimum charge means you can be charged fifty dollars for a two-dollar item!

List the approximate shipment lead time from each source and what they charge for priority shipments. Include the names, telephone numbers, and rates of shipping companies who offer overnight delivery.

Much of this information will come from service seminars. You will learn which parts are critical and which ones have a high failure rate, enabling you to establish guidelines for your parts inventory. You will also learn what special tools you will need for maintenance and repairs.

There is no substitute for being well prepared. With a little forethought, most problems can be solved in a short time, with a minimum amount of trouble.

PARTS WARRANTIES

Repair parts usually carry a warranty. Before you install a replacement part, attach a piece of masking tape to it and mark on it the following information:

1. Source
2. Invoice number
3. Invoice date
4. Shipping date
5. Date received
6. Date installed

If the part fails, you can quickly determine if it is under warranty. You won't have to spend a lot of time searching your files.

The thought of having to repair coin laundry machinery scares most inexperienced laundry owners, and they have reason to worry if they don't prepare themselves for the task. Follow the simple guidelines in this chapter and you will be fully qualified to maintain and repair your equipment. You may even find it enjoyable.

21

ACCOUNTING

ONE OF THE BENEFITS of owning a self-service laundry is that you spend very little time and effort doing the accounting. This is especially true for an unattended laundry. Some coin laundry accounting systems consist of reams of ledger paper maintained by overzealous accountants. Others contain only a few figures penciled on notebook paper.

Too much system is a waste of time and money. On the other hand, you cannot exercise good management control if your bookkeeping is inadequate. A good accounting system for a self-service laundry should:

1. Conform to the laws of Federal, state, and local governments.
2. Provide a clear picture of the financial condition of the business.

3. Contain sufficient detail for effective management planning.
4. Give sufficient information to prepare the tax returns.

If your laundry is <u>unattended</u>, you should be able to maintain all of your records for an entire year on a single sheet of paper. You shouldn't need more than two hours each month to develop your monthly Profit Analysis. If it takes longer than this, your system is too complicated.

You'll need additional forms and procedures if your coin laundry is <u>attended</u>:

1. Calendar
2. Payroll Record
3. Cash Tally

THE CALENDAR

A calendar may sound like a simple item, but try operating without it and see what happens. Buy one that has large squares for recording information next to each date.

Businesses with one or more employees must keep track of various tax and information filing deadlines. Write these dates on your calendar:

- Employee paydays
- Quarterly payroll taxes
- Annual payroll taxes
- Federal annual reports
- State annual reports

Don't forget to include your own quarterly estimated income tax filing deadlines. Some states require self-service laundries to pay sales taxes. If your state is one of them, add these dates to your calendar. If you are required to pay property taxes, add these deadlines also.

Accounting

THE PAYROLL RECORD

As an employer, you must withhold taxes from your employees' wages and make quarterly payments to the Federal and state governments. In addition to this, most local governments require tax payments based on payroll. Record all your payroll tax information in the Payroll Record.

Most office supply stores sell Payroll Records in single sheets or wire binders. Before purchasing your Payroll Record, make sure it meets Federal, state, and local requirements. Most are easy to understand and simple to maintain. After awhile, you won't need more than 20 minutes for each payday.

Contact the Social Security Administration, the Internal Revenue Service, and your state and local taxing authorities. They will give you a package of tax instructions, rules, and forms known as "The Employer's Tax Package." Study this information before you set up your accounting system.

Some businesses pay their employees every week. Others pay every other week, bimonthly, or once a month. A bimonthly payroll reduces the amount of time you spend on record keeping. A monthly payroll would be even better but is usually not popular with employees.

Consider paying your employees on the 15th and the last day of the month. This simplifies your bookkeeping. If you pay weekly (or every other week), you must carry part of your payroll expenses over to the following month. This is time consuming because it means a lot of extra calculations.

THE CASH TALLY SHEET

The Cash Tally Sheet is a daily record of the hours that each employee worked. Employees fill it out at the beginning and end of each shift. Total the hours and record them in the Payroll Record at the end of each pay period.

The Cash Tally Sheet balances the money in the cash register at the beginning and end of each employee's work shift. If errors are made during a shift, they are immediately exposed and corrections can be made. This form makes it easy to place responsibility for an error.

Have your employees write receipts for all cash sales and cash payouts from the cash register. These receipts are summarized, recorded, and attached to the back of the Cash Tally Sheet at the end of each shift. Summarize this information at the end of the month and record it on the Profit Analysis. You can use the Cash Tally Sheet on page 247 if you have employees.

THE PROFIT ANALYSIS

The single most important management tool available to you is the Profit Analysis. It must be absolutely accurate since it is the basis for most of the important decisions you will make. The Profit Analysis format on pages 248 and 249 can be used for both attended and unattended laundries.

Your Profit Analysis will help you determine developing trends. It will help you measure the effectiveness of your advertising programs. When you make mistakes (and you will), your Profit Analysis will help you uncover them quickly—before too much damage is done. Corrections can be made immediately.

All of your records can be maintained on one large ledger sheet or on two smaller ones. This includes sales, expenses, and other necessary financial information for an entire year. Although the example above shows only the first quarter, your Profit Analysis will show all twelve months, four quarterly totals, and an annual total.

Revenue
Revenue from the washers and dryers is broken down into types. You can collect coins from any or all the coin boxes at any time during the month. Just remember to do two things if you want to maintain an accurate monthly Profit Analysis:

Accounting

CASH TALLY SHEET

Name_____ Date_____   Time In_____Time Out_____

Bills:						Bills:					
Ones	____	•	1	=	$_____	Ones	____	•	1	=	$_____
Twos	____	•	2	=	_____	Twos	____	•	2	=	_____
Fives	____	•	5	=	_____	Fives	____	•	5	=	_____
Tens	____	•	10	=	_____	Tens	____	•	10	=	_____
Twenties	____	•	20	=	_____	Twenties	____	•	20	=	_____
Fifties	____	•	50	=	_____	Fifties	____	•	50	=	_____
Hundreds	____	•	100	=	_____	Hundreds	____	•	100	=	_____
Coin:						**Coin:**					
Pennies		•	.01	=	_____	Pennies		•	.01	=	_____
Nickels		•	.05	=	_____	Nickels		•	.05	=	_____
Dimes		•	.10	=	_____	Dimes		•	.10	=	_____
Quarters		•	.25	=	_____	Quarters		•	.25	=	_____
Halves		•	.50	=	_____	Halves		•	.50	=	_____
Dollars		•	1.00	=	_____	Dollars		•	1.00	=	_____

Checks   _____   Checks   _____

Beginning Balance   Ending Balance
In Cash Register $_____   In Cash Register $_____

Less Payments For: Less Receipts From:
_____ $_____   Wash & Fold $_____
_____ _____   Mending   _____
_____ _____   Ironing   _____
_____ _____   Machine Rental   _____
                                               Chemical Sales   _____

   Total Payments $_____   Total Receipts $_____

Total $_____ = Total $_____

Employee Signature_____

---

1. Keep a record of the <u>amount</u> of money you collect and the <u>type</u> of machine it came from.
2. Collect, count, and record all the money (from all of the machines) at the end of the last day of each month.

PROFIT ANALYSIS

JONES SELF-SERVICE LAUNDRY-1988

	Jan.	Feb.	Mar.	First Quarter
Revenue				
Top Load Washers	$3,496.80	$2,923.20	$3,645.60	$10,065.60
Cycles	4.7	4.2	4.9	4.6
Front Load Washers	892.80	939.60	781.20	2,613.60
Cycles	2.4	2.7	2.1	2.4
Stack Dryers	1,884.80	1,902.40	2,132.80	5,920.00
Cycles	3.8	4.1	4.3	4.1
30 Lb. Dryers	576.60	582.90	595.20	1,754.70
Cycles	6.2	6.7	6.4	6.4
Total W-D Revenue	$6,851.00	$6,348.10	$7,154.80	$20,353.90
Cycles	4.0	4.0	4.2	4.1
Wash & Fold	786.75	968.45	989.15	2,744.35
Mending	86.47	102.38	91.18	280.03
Soft Drink	295.35	292.60	357.50	945.45
Snacks	262.80	256.80	298.00	817.60
Laundry Aids	239.75	222.25	250.25	712.25
Total Revenue	$8,522.12	$8,190.58	$9,140.88	$25,853.58
Cost Of Goods Sold				
Soft Drink	$187.72	$185.98	$227.23	$600.93
Snacks	210.24	205.44	238.40	654.08
Laundry Aids	119.87	111.12	125.12	356.11
Total Cost	$517.83	$502.54	$590.75	$1,611.12
Gross Profit	$8,004.29	$7,688.04	$8,550.13	$24,242.46
Expenses				
Natural Gas	$685.00	$660.84	$728.45	$2,074.29
Electricity	227.63	215.14	241.61	684.38
Water	144.32	124.30	147.64	416.26
Sewer	176.00	176.00	176.00	528.00
Total Utilities	$1,232.95	$1,176.28	$1,293.70	$3,702.93
Rent	1,803.75	1,803.75	1,803.75	5,411.25
Interest	802.04	792.40	782.68	2,377.12
Maintenance	31.46	31.19	50.40	113.05
Operating Supplies	42.14	15.16	51.08	108.38
Office Supplies	10.96	12.06	12.70	35.72
Mending Supplies	16.47	18.02	14.63	49.12
Wash & Fold Supplies	56.18	67.76	69.23	193.17
Payroll	551.29	551.29	605.20	1,707.78
Insurance	172.00	172.00	172.00	516.00
Advertising	95.00	95.00	95.00	285.00
Telephone	39.19	41.57	53.24	134.00
Miscellaneous	28.00	26.85	54.90	109.75
Total Paid Expenses	$4,881.43	$4,803.33	$5,058.51	$14,743.27

Accounting

Depreciation	915.00	915.00	915.00	2,745.00
Property Taxes	116.67	116.67	116.67	350.01
Payroll Taxes (13.65%)	91.73	91.73	100.46	283.92
Withholding Reserve	120.71	120.71	130.80	372.22
Net Profit	$1,878.75	$1,640.60	$2,228.69	$5,748.04
Minus Loan Principal	963.24	972.88	982.60	2,918.72
Plus Depreciation	915.00	915.00	915.00	2,745.00
Cash To Owner	$1,830.51	$1,582.72	$2,161.09	$5,574.32
Accumulated Tax Liability				
Property Taxes	$116.67	$233.34	$350.01	
Payroll Taxes	91.73	183.46	283.92	
Withholding Taxes	120.71	241.42	372.22	
Total Tax Liability	$329.11	$658.22	$1,006.15	
Accumulated Depreciation	$21,960.00	$22,875.00	$23,790.00	

Coin Laundries — Road to Financial Independence

If your coin laundry is attended, summarize the information from your Cash Tally Sheets at the end of the month. This provides the total monthly revenue from services, such as wash-and-fold or mending. Record the figures on your Profit Analysis.

Be sure to list the revenue from each of your services separately. By doing this, you can keep track of how much revenue each produces. If sales start to decline, you will know where to concentrate your advertising.

Machine Cycles

Determine the average cycles of each machine per day by type. Multiply the number of machines of each type by the price per cycle and the number of days that your laundry was open during the month. Divide this into the revenue produced by each type of machine during the month.

Let's look at the Profit Analysis for Jones' Self-Service Laundry. The average cycles for January were determined this way:

$$\frac{\text{Total Monthly Revenue From T.L. Washers}}{32 \text{ T.L. Washers} \cdot 75¢ \text{ Per Wash} \cdot 31 \text{ Days}} = \frac{\$3,496.80}{\$744.00} = 4.7$$

$$\frac{\text{Total Monthly Revenue From F.L. Washers}}{6 \text{ F.L. Washers} \cdot \$2.00 \text{ Per Wash} \cdot 31 \text{ Days}} = \frac{\$892.80}{\$372.00} = 2.4$$

$$\frac{\text{Total Monthly Revenue From Stacked Dryers}}{32 \text{ Dryers} \cdot 50¢ \text{ Per Dry Cycle} \cdot 31 \text{ Days}} = \frac{\$1,884.80}{\$496.00} = 3.8$$

$$\frac{\text{Total Monthly Revenue From 30 Lb. Dryers}}{6 \text{ Dryers} \cdot 50¢ \text{ Per Dry Cycle} \cdot 31 \text{ Days}} = \frac{\$576.60}{\$93.00} = 6.2$$

To get the average number of cycles per day for all the laundry equipment, use this formula:

$$\frac{\$3,496.80 + \$892.80 + \$1,884.80 + \$576.60}{\$744.00 + \$372.00 + \$496.00 + \$93.00} = \frac{\$6,851.00}{\$1,705.00} = 4.0$$

Accounting

Notice that the top-loading washers get twice the use of the front-loaders. Perhaps $2.00 a wash is too high, or maybe the customers don't know how to work the front-loading washers and need help.

Jones should place more emphasis on the front-loading washers in her promotions, emphasizing their ability to wash rugs, sleeping bags, bedspreads, and other large items. This will add new customers and increase revenue from the front-loaders.

Notice that the stacked dryers are not producing enough revenue. The single-load top-loading washers average 4.7 cycles per day, but the single-load stacked dryers average only 3.8 cycles. Notice also that the 30-pound-capacity dryers are averaging 6.2 cycles per day while the 35-pound-capacity front-loading washers are averaging only 2.4 cycles.

Jones' customers clearly prefer the big-load dryers to the single-load ones, probably because they can dry three times more clothes in the large dryers for the same amount of money. If Jones reduces the amount of drying time per quarter (25¢) on the large dryers, total dryer revenue will increase immediately.

In January, Jones' Self-Service Laundry achieved an overall monthly average of 4 cycles per day. Washers and dryers produced revenue of $6,851.00. Equipment cycles should be watched carefully. A downward trend means trouble, and steps must then be taken to increase business.

Cost Of Goods Sold

Be sure to list costs of goods sold by category. This way you can keep track of the profit on each item you sell and know when it starts to decline. Don't hesitate to make periodic price adjustments to maintain your profit goals. We are all subject to inflation.

Expenses

At the end of each month, assemble all your expense information from your check record, the Cash Tally Sheets, and your Payroll Record. Post the expenses in the proper expense category of your Profit Analysis.

Make a separate total for the utilities so that you can check these ratios: (See "Pricing" on page 179.)

$$\frac{\text{Rent}}{\text{Washer \& Dryer Revenue}} = \frac{\$1,804}{\$6,851} = 26.3\%$$

$$\frac{\text{Utilities}}{\text{Washer \& Dryer Revenue}} = \frac{\$1,233}{\$6,851} = 18.0\%$$

Remember, your rent should not be more than 25 percent of washer/dryer receipts, or utilities more than 20 percent. January rent was only 1.3 percent <u>above</u> this guideline. Total utilities were 2 percent <u>under</u>. On the average, these two major expenses were not out of line.

Depreciation, Property Taxes, Payroll Taxes, Withholding Reserve

Notice that depreciation, property taxes, payroll taxes, and the withholding reserve are listed at the bottom of the expense column on the Profit Analysis, not included in "Total Paid Expenses." That's because no cash was paid for any of these expenses during the month.

You have to offset depreciation by profits. Even though no cash is paid out, the wear-and-tear on Jones' equipment is costing her $915 every month. This reduces her net profit. Review the method for determining depreciation on pages 39–40, and pages 187–188.

Property taxes are normally paid annually. Although no cash is paid out in the meantime, you become liable for a portion of your property taxes each month. If you don't deduct this liability each month, your net profit figure will be inaccurate.

Jones figured her payroll taxes at 13.65 percent of the hourly wages by adding the individual percentage rates for these taxes:

Accounting

- Federal Social Security Tax-Employer's Portion
- Federal Unemployment Tax
- State Unemployment Tax
- Worker's Compensation
- Local Excise Tax

Although payroll taxes are paid quarterly, they are a liability against the business. This liability increases each hour that an employee works. Consider payroll taxes each month when figuring net profit.

The withholding reserve is the amount of taxes that Jones must withhold from her employees' wages. The total payroll expense for January was $672.00. Only $551.29 was paid directly to the employee during the month. The balance of $120.71 must be paid to the taxing authorities at a future date and is listed separately.

Net Profit

Get net profit by subtracting the expenses from the gross profit. Expenses include monthly payments shown as "Total Paid Expenses." They also include depreciation and tax liabilities for the month, even though they may be paid later.

Suppose Jones' business began on January 1 and then was permanently shut down at the end of the month. Jones would have to pay a total of $116.67 for property taxes, $91.73 for payroll taxes, and $120.71 that was withheld from employees' wages. This money would come from the gross profit in January.

Available Cash

Jones figures how much cash she can take out of her business by deducting the "principal" portion of her loan payment from the net profit and then adding back the depreciation.

Accumulated Tax Liability

As a management aid, tax liabilities are summarized in the Profit Analysis. Suppose Jones maintains a minimum checkbook balance of $800 and withdraws $1,830.51 from the business in January. Looking at the checkbook reconciliation below, you can see there's $329.11 left in the checking account to pay taxing authorities at a future date.

CHECKBOOK RECONCILIATION

Checkbook Balance January 1st		$800.00
January Deposits		8,522.12
Total Available Cash		$9,322.12
Deductions From Checkbook Balance:		
Payments For Merchandise	$517.83	
Payments For Expenses	4,881.43	
Loan Principal Payment	963.24	
Owner Withdrawals	1,830.51	
Total Deductions		8,193.01
Checkbook Balance February 1st		$1,129.11
Minimum Checkbook Balance		$800.00
Accumulated Tax Liability		329.11
Total		$1,129.11

March shows a total tax liability of $1,006.15. Part of the payroll taxes and all the withholding taxes will be paid sometime in April. At the end of April, the March balance of $1,006.15 will decrease by the amounts that have been paid out. It will be increased by the April tax liability.

Simple, isn't it? It will be after you work with it. You should always know how much money you need in your bank account to cover future liabilities. A quick glance at your Profit Analysis will tell you.

Accounting

REVIEW YOUR PROFIT PICTURE

Many business people place so much emphasis on revenue that they fail to manage expenses. Profit suffers. It's nice to see revenues increase, but you'd probably settle for fewer sales if it meant more profit. An analysis of Jones' Self-Service Laundry illustrates this point:

First Quarter Revenue Generated By The Employee:		
Wash & Fold Service		$2,744.35
Mending		280.03
Total Revenue		$3,024.38
Expenses Related To The Production Of This Revenue:		
Utilities	$127.72	
Maintenance	10.00	
Operating Supplies	38.00	
Office Supplies	20.00	
Mending Supplies	49.12	
Wash & Fold Supplies	193.17	
Payroll	2,080.00	
Insurance	46.00	
Telephone	134.00	
Payroll Taxes	283.92	
Total Expenses		2,981.93
Profit Generated By Employee		$42.45

Jones' employee generated a profit of $42.45 in three months. This doesn't justify the time and effort it took to manage that employee. To increase profits, Jones should:

- Decrease employee-related expenses
- Decrease service-related expenses
- Increase sales of existing services
- Add services

If the profit generated by the employee cannot be increased, it may be best to convert the laundry to an unattended one. Jones could then concentrate her time and effort on increasing washer and dryer cycles. Profits would be likely to increase considerably.

A vending machine or video game would produce more profit than the employee—with less aggravation. A new vending machine would cost less than the employee expenses Jones paid during the first quarter.

Another alternative (see pages 209–210) would be to sublease part of the space to another entrepreneur who could conduct a wash-and-fold service, mending, or other services that would be mutually beneficial.

TAKE CARE OF YOUR ACCOUNTANT

Any accountant can tell you about business owners who come in with boxes of unorganized paper right before the tax deadline, expecting their taxes to be filed on time. The head of one accounting firm says "We do it, and we do it on time. But they pay for it. Boy, do they pay for it!" A word to the wise!

This accounting system is only one of many that you can use. No matter which system you choose, it should meet all legal requirements, be a good management tool, and provide sufficient information for your income tax returns.

Your accountant will set up your depreciation schedules according to Federal and state law. Once this has been done, the accounting system laid out here will provide all the information needed to prepare your returns. This information is summarized on a single sheet of paper, and charges should be reasonable.

22

CONSERVING ENERGY

THE SHARP RISE in energy costs in the last decade has significantly impacted on the coin-operated laundry industry. Energy costs are a major expense. Your profit will depend a great deal on how well you control them.

This is especially true if you are running an old laundry with aging, outdated equipment. Total utility costs (natural gas, electricity, water, and sewer) in some of these old laundries can run as high as 50 percent of gross receipts. Much of this expense is for natural gas and electricity.

DEVELOPING AN ENERGY-SAVINGS PROGRAM

Make it a challenge to reduce energy expenses. Here's how to start:

- List areas where you can reduce energy costs.
- List possible solutions for each problem area.

- Analyze each solution.
- Pick the best solution for each problem.
- Develop a time schedule for putting each measure into effect.

Give your program some thought so that you don't spend $100 to save $50. Get all the facts about a proposed energy-saving measure so you can determine the true benefits.

Contact your gas and electric companies. Most offer energy audits and recommendations for reducing energy costs. These audits can be had for free or a nominal fee. It's a good place to start your energy-savings program.

INVESTIGATING ENERGY-SAVING PROPOSALS

Recently, an entire industry has developed around energy savings. This includes consulting and engineering firms and manufacturers of every conceivable type of energy-saving device. As a laundry owner, you will be constantly contacted by sales-people selling energy-saving devices.

Be careful! Every new industry has its share of opportunists. Some devices will have as much affect on energy savings as Dr. Zarcon's Snake Oil has in curing cancer. Don't be victimized by high-pressure salespeople. Ask for a list of users, and check with each.

Always contact the Better Business Bureau or other consumer protection groups before signing an order. Never make a down-payment before you thoroughly investigate the manufacturer and the product. Try to get the manufacturer to provide a written guarantee of the savings, and make sure you agree on how the savings will be measured.

THE COST OF ENERGY-SAVING MEASURES

There are many measures you can take to save energy, ranging from a few dollars worth of insulation to energy-saving devices costing thousands of dollars. To a large extent, the cost of these measures will depend on your knowledge and skill.

Most people can insulate a hot water tank, but how many can design, build, and install an air-return system for a dryer? If you can design and build exhaust-vent efficiency devices or a waste-water heat exchanger, you can save thousands of dollars. Approach energy savings as a "do-it-yourself" project whenever possible.

ESTABLISHING PRIORITIES

Set up a timetable for your energy-saving measures. Use this formula to find out how many months it will take you to recover your cost:

$$\frac{\text{Dollar Cost Of System,}}{\text{Proven Dollar Savings}} = \frac{\text{Number Of Months Required}}{\text{To Recover The Cost}}$$
$$\text{Per Month}$$

Establish your priorities based on how quickly each pays for itself from the savings it creates. For example, one system might pay for itself in 8 months. Another, 18 months. Obviously you'll install the system with an 8-month cost recovery first.

Solar panels can save on water heating costs. Suppose it takes 33 months for the savings to equal the cost of the system. If your lease expires in 30 months, there would be no savings. In fact, there would be a sizeable loss. *Always consider the length of your lease before making an improvement.*

ENERGY-SAVING MEASURES

Heating and Air Conditioning

Adding insulation to your building (or leased space) and installing tamper-proof thermostats can save on heating and air conditioning costs. In some climates, you can save by replacing the furnace and air conditioner with a heat pump. In most climates, you can replace the air conditioner with the more economical evaporative cooler.

Eliminating Utility Sinks

Utility sinks produce no income, and they are vulnerable to vandalism. Eliminate them, particularly if your laundry is unattended. Children play in them and waste (hot) water. Transients use them to wash themselves as well as their clothes.

Many laundries have utility sinks without automatic shutoff valves. Water can run in these sinks for many hours before someone bothers to turn it off. If it's hot water, look out gas bill!

Conserving Electricity

Motors that run on 220 volts cost less to operate than 120-volt motors. Manufacturers often give you an option. If you are building a new laundry, specify the more efficient 220-volt motors. If you are replacing old equipment, be sure the cost to rewire for 220-volt electrical service doesn't exceed the savings.

Laundries with large window areas don't require full lighting on bright days. Ceiling fixtures can be wired (or easily rewired) to provide 50 percent illumination. For example, a laundry with 20 four-tube fixtures would contain 80 forty-watt fluorescent tubes using a total of 3,200 watts of electricity per hour. Fifty percent illumination would save 1,600 watts per hour.

Suppose the laundry could be operated at 50 percent illumination for 12 hours a day in the summer. Calculate the savings for the month of July at a rate of 6.03¢ per kwh (1,000 watts) of electricity:

$$\frac{31 \text{ Days} \cdot 12 \text{ Hours} \cdot 1{,}600 \text{ Watts}}{1{,}000 \text{ Watts}} \cdot \$.0603 = \$35.89$$

Many businesses operate their exterior electric signs 24 hours per day. A few changes can reduce operating costs by 50 to 70 percent. Rewire your sign to provide 50 percent illumination, and install a simple light-sensor in the circuit. This will increase the light at night and during overcast days. Install a timer to turn the sign off automatically when the laundry is closed.

Using Energy-Efficient Washers

Replace worn-out washers with new, energy-efficient machines. New washers use cold-water rinses instead of hot or warm-water rinses. This can reduce your hot water consumption by as much as 55 percent!

Sometimes old washers can be altered to make them more energy efficient. On some makes, you can replace the timers and/or water-temperature selection-switches with newer parts that eliminate costly warm-water rinses.

Some washer timers can be altered to change the temperature of the rinse water from warm to cold. This saves a lot of money that would be spent for new timers. It also requires a lot of knowledge and skill on your part.

Using Energy-Efficient Dryers

Clothes dryers pull cold air past a gas burner (or electric heating element) where it is heated. The heated air is then pushed (or pulled) through the revolving drum, where it evaporates moisture from the clothes. The moisture-laden heated air is then exhausted out the back of the dryer.

Cycling-thermostats maintain the temperature of the air inside the dryer drum. They turn the burner (or element) on when the temperature reaches a predetermined minimum and off when the predetermined maximum temperature is reached. The colder the supply-air, the more the burner (or element) cycles and consumes energy. Energy use increases in winter.

You can make clothes dryers more efficient by:

- Supplying air at a warmer temperature
- Reducing heat loss from the dryer

Newer energy-efficient dryers recirculate part of the heated exhaust-air past the burner (or element) and back through the dryer drum. In addition to this, the energy-wasting continuous-burning pilots on gas dryers have been replaced by automatic ignition systems. Considerable savings result when these changes are made to older style dryers.

Some coin laundry owners preheat the supply-air to their dryers. They route the dryer exhaust-vent inside the supply-air intake-duct. The supply-air is preheated by the exhaust-air duct. The supply-air intake-duct is then insulated to reduce heat loss.

In many coin laundries, the tops, sides and backs of the dryers are exposed to an unheated area. Insulating these surfaces with noncombustible insulation prevents heat loss. This saves energy by reducing the number of times the burner (or element) must cycle to maintain temperature.

If you vent your dryers properly and have a sufficient supply of air, they will operate efficiently. If you are using gas dryers, save money by maintaining clean, properly adjusted burners. Use these tips! You will reduce energy costs considerably.

THE WATER HEATING SYSTEM

Water heating systems use a lot of energy, so they provide a lot of opportunities to conserve energy. This is especially true in older laundries. You can usually reduce energy consumption by modifying the water heating system.

Insulating The Water Tank

Insulate the top, bottom, and sides of your hot-water tank. The more insulation, the better. Consider that a 375-gallon water tank has over 70 square feet of steel surface. This is comparable to a 7-foot by 10-foot glass window. A considerable amount of heat is lost if the surface is not insulated.

Water heaters that have the heater and tank combined generally have some insulation between the tank and the outer steel wrap. Adding an insulation blanket around the outer cover is inexpensive and reduces heat loss even more.

Reducing Water Temperature

When energy was cheap, the temperature of hot water in coin laundries was rarely below 145°F. Some maintained temperatures of 185° or more. You can save a considerable amount of money by lowering the water temperature. Temperatures of 115°F. to 120°F. will produce steam when the washer is filling, satisfying most customers.

You can calculate your savings this way:

$$\text{B.t.u. Savings} = \frac{\text{Gallons Of Hot Water Per Month} \cdot \text{8.345 Lb. Per Gallon} \cdot \text{Temperature Reduction}}{\text{Water Heater Efficiency}}$$

First, determine your monthly hot water usage and the efficiency-factor of your water heater. The water heater specification sheet should provide the heater efficiency-factor. If not, contact the manufacturer.

If you will recall, as a nationwide average the hot wash is selected 34 percent of the time and the warm wash, 53 percent of the time. Review your specification sheets. If your washers use 16 gallons of hot water on the hot wash setting and 8 gallons on the warm wash setting, the average hot water usage would be 9.68 gallons per cycle (34% of 16, plus 53% of 8). (See page 85 for review.)

Suppose your laundry contained 24 washers. If they averaged 5 cycles per day in January, your hot water consumption would be 36,010 gallons for the month (9.68 gal. • 5 cycles • 24 washers • 31 days). Suppose your heater efficiency-factor is 75 percent and you lower your water temperature 25°. Using the above formula, calculate the B.t.u. savings:

$$\frac{36{,}010 \text{ Gal.} \cdot 8.345 \text{ Lb. Per Gal.} \cdot 25°F.}{.75} = 10{,}016{,}781 \text{ B.t.u.}$$

Now look at your gas bill to convert the B.t.u. savings to dollars. If you are paying 46.887¢ per therm (100,000 B.t.u.), your savings is $46.97 for the month. Dividing 10,016,781 B.t.u. by 100,000 gives you 100.17 therms of gas. Multiply this savings by your rate of $.46887 per therm. You get $46.97 in savings for the month of January. It's all profit!

Eliminating Water Recirculating Systems

Washing machines fill with a measured amount of water. If the water in the hot water lines has been sitting for a while and is cold, that is what the customer will get. Hot water recirculating systems are sometimes installed to insure that hot water is delivered to the washers. These systems continuously recirculate hot water from the tank, through the lines and back to the tank.

These systems are a service to the customer, but there is considerable heat loss. Don't use them unless the hot water lines between the heater and the washers are exceptionally long. You can find this out by figuring the amount of water in the line between the water tank and the farthermost washer.

Calculate the gallons of water per foot of pipe by squaring the inside diameter (inches) and multiplying the result by .0408. Suppose there is 30 feet of 1½-inch water line between your water tank and the last washer. It would contain only 2.75 gallons (1.5 • 1.5 • .0408 • 30 feet). If it takes 16 gallons to fill a washer, don't bother with a recirculating system.

Insulating Hot Water Lines

You <u>must</u> insulate hot water lines if you have a hot water recirculating system. Otherwise, you may by providing a service to your customers, but you will waste a lot of energy. When providing hot water in the range of 115°F. to 120°F., fully-insulated hot water lines will prevent a lot of complaints.

Some coin laundry owners insulate the cold water lines. Water condenses on uninsulated cold water lines in warm, humid weather. When it drips from overhead cold water pipes, it can ruin the ceiling. Insulating these pipes also helps to prevent them from freezing in very cold weather.

Maintaining And Modifying Your Water Heater

Proper maintenance of your water heater can do a lot to conserve energy. Periodically clean the burners and check the adjustment. Delime your heater on a regular schedule. (Follow the directions in the water heater service-manual.) If your water heater has a continuous burning pilot, remove it and install an automatic pilot.

Rapid cycling of the burner is required to maintain water temperature during slow periods. This is highly inefficient and wastes energy. Install a timer on your water heater. Set it so it will shut the heater off during regular slow periods of the business day and when the laundry is closed. Any demand for hot water can be supplied from the hot water storage tank.

Preheating Water Heater Supply-Water

Preheating water heater supply-water by passive means has been the focus of many laundry owners in recent years. A small coin laundry will use over 36,000 gallons of hot water per month. It requires a lot of energy to heat this much water!

Suppose you pay 47¢ per therm for natural gas. You would save approximately $1.88 per month for every Fahrenheit degree that the supply-water could be raised by passive means. A 20° increase in supply-water temperature would reduce natural gas usage by about 25 percent. That's substantial!

Don't forget that the savings must justify the cost of the system, including installation and maintenance. Let's look at some passive water heating systems that are used in coin laundries:

- **Solar**—Solar panels are used to heat supply-water. The panels are generally mounted on the roof, provided the roof deck is designed to accept the added weight.

- **Waste-Water Heat Exchanger**—Washer waste-water is pumped to a large holding tank on the way to the main sewer. The holding tank contains coils, through which the supply-water passes on the way to the water heater. The warmer waste-water increases the temperature of the supply-water.

- **Dryer Mounted Heat Exchanger**—Coils are mounted near the burners on clothes dryers. Supply-water passes through these coils and is preheated before entering the water heater. Although the temperature of the supply-water is increased, the efficiency of the dryer is decreased to some extent because the cold supply-water has a cooling effect on the dryer.

- **Exhaust Gas Heat Exchangers**—These heat exchangers are mounted in the exhaust-air ducts of the dryers and/or the hot water heater. Supply-water is preheated as it passes through the coils on the way to the water heater.

- **Subterranean Heat Exchangers**—Heat exchanger coils are placed deep in the ground where the temperature is stable at around 55°F. Supply water passes through these coils and is heated to 55°F. This system is effective only if the underground temperature is significantly higher than the temperature of the supply-water. This system is expensive, which may cancel out the benefits.

Surprisingly, some of the most effective energy-saving measures are the least expensive. Many of these have been mentioned in this chapter.

The energy industry is changing rapidly. If you want to stay informed, attend trade shows and subscribe to the various trade publications. Listen to the equipment salespeople who call at your coin laundry. And visit other coin laundries to see what owners there are doing to reduce energy costs.

Conserving Energy

Remember, don't purchase an energy-saving device before you fully understand how it works. Don't purchase an energy-saving device until you have verified the dollar savings. And don't base the value of an energy-saving device on energy savings alone. You might find yourself paying $1,500 for a $50 piece of equipment.

Men are able to trust one another, knowing the exact degree of dishonesty they are entitled to expect.

—Stephen Butler Leacock

Trust everybody, but cut the cards.

—Finley Peter Dunne

Never do something you do not approve of in order more quickly to accomplish something you do approve of, for there are no safe short-cuts in piloting a business.

—John Pierpont Morgan

23

MANAGING
YOUR LAUNDRY

CORPORATIONS ARE FULL of high-paid executives who can't manage. They sometimes hang on for years. But an entrepreneur who is a bad manager is unlikely to survive very long. Survival time is usually measured in months.

If you could stack all the quarters on edge that are collected from a well-managed, medium-size coin laundry in a single month, they would reach 1,000 feet higher than the world's tallest building. Customer satisfaction is the key to this kind of volume. The customer always rules.

MAINTAINING A CLEAN LAUNDRY

The biggest concern of most coin laundry customers is cleanliness. New coin laundries are clean and attractive to customers. Unfortunately, many of them are allowed to gradually deteriorate. As a result, the good customers go elsewhere.

Rundown laundries attract undesirable, destructive customers This type of customer will cause further deterioration. Be as critical of your laundry as the famous white-glove inspectors in the military. When it comes to cleanliness, a laundry that is less than perfect is going to lose customers—guaranteed.

MAINTAINING YOUR EQUIPMENT

Cleanliness is the first management priority, but maintenance runs a close second. Coin laundry customers are highly critical of laundries with a large number of "out-of-order" signs on the equipment. When your equipment breaks down, repair it as soon as possible. Don't forget that idle equipment makes no money.

Be sure to make refunds to customers who lose money. If your laundry is unattended, maintain a "Refund & Suggestion Box." The box is locked and has a slot in the top. Your customers can get a refund by filling out the refund-card and dropping it into the box. As to the suggestions, you'll find that some of them make interesting reading.

KEEPING YOUR VENDING MACHINES FULL

Keep your vending machines well-stocked with merchandise and your bill changer well-stocked with coin. This may seem obvious, but take a tour of coin laundries. You'll find poorly managed ones with empty soap dispensers, candy dispensers, and pop machines. You will even find empty bill changers. There is no excuse for this. Nothing frustrates a customer more than not being able to get change.

KNOWING YOUR CUSTOMERS

Make friends with your customers. Know them by name. This is especially important if your laundry is unattended. Customers don't usually victimize friends. If your customers like you, they will be a deterrent to vandals.

Managing Your Laundry

Self-service laundry customers spend 1½ to 2 hours washing, drying, and folding their clothes. If your laundry is unattended, you can still meet most of your customers. Make short, frequent visits to your laundry to clean the premises, stock the vending machines, and check the equipment.

HANDLING CUSTOMER COMPLAINTS

Customer complaints are a part of doing business. If you learn how to handle them properly, you will build good customer relations and your business will grow. Improperly handled complaints drive customers off. Sometimes an improperly handled complaint will even lead to vandalism.

When customers have complaints, listen without interrupting. Acknowledge their point of view and thank them for bringing the problem to your attention. Act on the complaint whenever possible, and quickly. It costs less to keep a customer than it does to find a new one. Satisfied customers are good advertising, and they usually result in increased business.

AVOID GIVING ADVICE

Inexperienced laundry owners have a tendency to offer customers advice on proper laundry procedures. Customers are usually put off by this. Don't offer advice unless your customer asks for it. The exception is when your customer's laundry procedure is likely to damage your equipment.

Sometimes a customer will ask you for advice on how to launder a specific garment. Be careful! You will be blamed if it turns out badly.

Most garments have a tag on an inside seam which gives the manufacturer's recommendations for cleaning or laundering. When you are asked for advice, point this tag out to your customer. Then if the customer is dissatisfied with the results, it's the manufacturer's fault.

MAINTAINING AN EQUIPMENT-READY LAUNDRY

Some customers leave their clothes in the machines, some-times for long periods of time, after the cycle is complete. They start the machines and then go shopping or run errands. This can be a major problem, particularly in unattended laundries, because it aggravates other customers who want to use those machines. It also reduces machine cycles, and this reduces your profit.

Place signs near the washers and dryers that tell the cycle length in minutes. This helps reduce the amount of idle time. Council with customers who repeatedly use your machines for storage. You may even have to remove their clothes. It's better to offend a few problem customers than to lose machine cycles on busy days.

Signs like these help prevent problems:

```
CLOTHES LEFT UNATTENDED

ARE SUBJECT TO THEFT
```

```
CLOTHES LEFT UNATTENDED

WILL BE REMOVED

CALL 373–4829 TO RECLAIM
```

USING INSTRUCTIONAL SIGNS

Signs are important in a self-service coin laundry, particularly if it is unattended. Using humor gets your message across without sacrificing good will. Here are some examples:

SUPPORT YOUR LOCAL THIEF

(LEAVE YOUR CLOTHES UNATTENDED)

MACHINE MALFUNCTION???

DON'T BRUISE THE MACHINE
BRUISE THE OWNER

FILL OUT A REFUND CARD AND <u>MAKE HIM PAY</u>

UNATTENDED CHILDREN

MAY BE TOWED

AT OWNER'S EXPENSE

ELIMINATING A NUISANCE

Self-service laundries are occasionally plagued by a nuisance—an incorrigible customer. Fortunately this is rare. But a customer like this can adversely affect your business by driving off good customers. Get rid of him—politely. When gentle persuasion fails, you may have to use stronger measures.

Filthy language has become "freedom of speech" and lewd behavior has become "freedom of expression." Supposedly this is guaranteed by the Constitution. Consult your attorney before taking action. Physically throwing someone out of your laundry may be morally right and justified. But it may also be illegal. It could get you sued.

ABANDONED CLOTHING

Abandoned clothing is a by-product of coin-operated laundries. The amount of clothing that is abandoned in a medium-size high-volume laundry can fill a small storage room in three months. The quality of the clothing will range from rags to high-fashion expensive garments.

Your attorney can tell you if the law requires you to hold abandoned items for a specific time before disposing of them. Many businesses post signs stating that the laundry owner is not responsible for loss or theft. The law may say otherwise.

Develop a system for handling abandoned clothing. You can inventory, package, and date each load of abandoned clothes and then retain them for a specific time period, such as three months. When the clothes are claimed, the customer pays for washing, drying, packaging, storing, and labeling them. Unclaimed clothes can be sold at a "garage sale" or donated to a nonprofit organization.

Ask for positive identification before returning abandoned clothes. Have your customer sign a receipt containing the name, address, telephone number, and the date. List and describe the returned articles.

Managing Your Laundry

Never put abandoned clothing on the clothes-folding tables to wait to be claimed. This clutters your laundry and inconveniences your customers. It also invites theft.

PREPARING AN EMPLOYEE MANUAL

If your laundry is attended, develop an "Employee Rules & Procedures Manual." The contents will depend on your objectives and the number and types of services that you plan to offer. Include a detailed description of the employees' cleaning duties in the manual.

Give a copy of it to each employee to read and sign. Review the contents of the manual with each employee on a regular basis.

SUPERVISING YOUR EMPLOYEES

Attended self-service laundries require as much if not more supervision than unattended laundries. When attendants are left to themselves, they tend to develop every bad habit imaginable. Here's a list of the most common problems that arise when attendants are not properly managed:

- Theft of money, products, or supplies
- Theft of customers' possessions
- Nonperformance of job duties
- Personal use of business telephone
- Personal use of laundry facilities or services
- Misuse of cigarettes, food, and reading material
- Socializing with customers
- Allowing personal items to clutter the premises
- Improper dress and poor personal appearance
- Deterioration of attitude

If some of these points seem trivial, consider the plight of one unfortunate business owner. His employee ran up a bill for $9,867.38 on a social-talk party-line, which the owner refused to pay. He was taken to court. Not only did the court rule that the owner had to pay the bill, but he was sued again by the employee after he fired him!

Make random frequent visits to your laundry so your employees cannot prepare for them. Look for problems during each visit. If you find a problem, point it out. Give your employee specific directions on how to correct it. Be sure to follow up on it during your next surprise visit.

Severely criticizing your employees can make their lives miserable and ruin potentially good employees. Always temper your criticism with understanding. Be sure to praise employees who perform well.

Coin laundry attendants have a significant impact on customer relations. A well-dressed, well-mannered attendant with a positive attitude will increase business. A disorderly attendant with a bad attitude will drive customers off. This can eventually ruin you.

USING A PROFESSIONAL SHOPPING SERVICE

You might consider using a professional shopping service periodically. They send people posing as customers to your store to determine firsthand how employees treat your customers. The shopping agency then provides you with a written report on the findings. Learning of an employee who treats customers badly justifies the expense for this service.

You may feel that this is equivalent to spying on your employees. Remember, your money is at stake! If you don't exercise tight management control, your profits will suffer.

24

HIRING PROFESSIONAL ASSISTANCE

YOU ARE A HIGHLY unusual person if you can start and operate a successful self-service laundry without any professional help. Don't try it! You'll make costly mistakes if you do. At the very least, you will need an attorney. You may also need the services of an accountant, an engineer, and a consultant.

THE ATTORNEY

Your attorney can help you determine whether your business will be a corporation, a partnership, or a proprietorship by explaining the advantages and disadvantages of each. Your attorney can also be useful by handling the necessary paperwork for the Federal, state, and local governments.

If you sign contracts without consulting your attorney, you may eventually be faced with a costly problem that you cannot solve. A serious problem could even mean the end of your business! By this point, your attorney is of no help unless the provisions of the contract are illegal.

Sometimes you can renegotiate a bad contract. If the contract is legal, however, you have no _real_ basis for negotiation. You can only hope that the contract holder is compassionate, but don't count on this.

Be sure to have your attorney review all contracts before you sign them, including purchase agreements, sales contracts, construction contracts, and your lease. It's much less costly to prevent legal problems than to cure them. If you let your attorney review contracts before you sign them, and a problem develops, he will be defending _his_ work—not yours.

You are responsible for making decisions. Don't rely on your attorney for that. You are responsible for formulating business policy. You attorney tells you if your policies are legal.

When you develop a contract, _you_ decide what goes in it. Let your attorney word it. In short, you decide what to do, and your attorney tells you how to do it with the least amount of legal exposure.

THE ACCOUNTANT

The majority of people who itemize deductions have an accountant prepare their income tax forms. In the past, many people viewed these services as a convenience. Since the so called "simplification" of the tax laws in 1987, what was once a convenience is now a necessity.

If your coin laundry is a proprietorship, you can establish a simple accounting system like the one described in Chapter 21. You may still want your accountant to set the procedures up for you. The accounting for a partnership or a corporation is more complex and legally sensitive. In this case, get your accountant and your attorney involved.

Don't try to complicate a simple business. Keep your accounting procedures basic. You should be able to maintain your own records once you set up your accounting system. Paying for monthly or quarterly accounting services just creates additional expenses. And expenses are the enemy of your profits.

THE ENGINEER

Government authorities sometimes require that an engineer prepares the plans and specifications for a new coin-operated laundry. Fees can run as much as 20-percent (or more) of the cost of the entire project. This can be $30,000 for a medium-size laundry. It's impossible to justify these charges for a project as simple as a coin laundry.

Can these costs be reduced? Sometimes. Even if the law requires that an engineer prepares your plans and specifications, prepare them yourself with the help of your subcontractors. When the plans are complete, find a cooperative engineer who will put his stamp on your plans and specifications for a modest fee. Remember to keep it thorough, but simple.

THE CONSULTANT

Small business owners have a tendency to develop tunnel vision. They lose sight of the overall picture, and the business suffers. One of the most valuable (and overlooked) sources of professional help is the consultant. A good consultant will pay for himself by helping you to avoid many costly mistakes.

A good consultant can save you thousands. And the fee is usually a small fraction of this. Since the cost for professional consulting depends more on how the consultant is used than on the hourly rate, it's important to understand how to make effective use of a consultant.

Consultants give advice. They do not get involved in the daily operation of your business. Don't hire a consultant to police your job site for three months while your laundry is under construction. A consultant is not a general contractor. Don't expect a good consultant to select your equipment. That's your responsibility.

Coin Laundries — Road to Financial Independence

What a good consultant does is to provide you with help in making your decisions. Their value lies in their experience and objectivity. They suggest a number of solutions to a particular problem. You pick the one that best meets your needs.

If possible, find a consultant who is experienced in the self-service laundry industry. This way, much of the consulting can be done over the telephone, saving you money. Points can be expanded upon by follow-up letters.

Pick a consultant who offers computerized spreadsheet analysis. This is especially critical during the first two years of your new business when mistakes can mean the difference between success and failure. Using computerized spreadsheet analysis, a consultant experienced in the self-service laundry business can point out weaknesses and offer a variety of remedies.

Always check the reputation of any professional assistance you hire. Contractors, engineers, attorneys, accountants, and consultants can also be dishonest or inept. This can lead to disaster. Thoroughly interview these people before hiring them. Your investment is at stake!

25

GETTING STARTED

YOU CAN BECOME financially independent by owning and operating coin laundries, but you cannot do it overnight. Developing a business is like growing a tree—it takes time. Be patient. Spend whatever time it takes to achieve your goals.

To make a lot of money, you need to own and operate several profitable laundries. Make big plans, but be sure you carry them out in stages that are simple and easy; ones that won't overwhelm you. Man has covered great distances by placing one foot in front of the other—repeatedly.

Begin by looking for a good location for your first self-service laundry. Take your time and find the best location possible. Remember, location is the single most important factor for the success of a coin laundry.

While you are looking for a location, be sure to start contacting possible sources for financing. (It's never too early to start developing these sources.) Cultivate a good working relationship with the loan officers. Their knowledge and experience will be helpful. And you need all the help you can get.

You may find that several locations look good. Review Chapter 7 and be sure to do a thorough market survey of each. Use this information to pick the best location for your first coin laundry. You'll be glad you did.

Study this book carefully as you progress with your plans. Before making a commitment, carefully study the chapter(s) covering that step. Don't worry about wearing out the book. We'll sell you another.

When the problems seem insurmountable and you wonder why you started the project in the first place, take time off. Your mind is telling you that it needs a rest. Don't make excuses that you can't afford to get away. You can't afford <u>not</u> to! When you return, those "insurmountable" problems will will be much easier to solve.

Finally, I've had a lot of fun writing this book. I hope it brings you pleasure and helps you achieve your goals. If is does, share your success by sending a picture of your coin laundry.

ASSOCIATIONS AND PUBLICATIONS

THE FOLLOWING is a list of associations and publications whose advertising and articles deal primarily with the coin-operated laundry and dry-cleaning industry:

Coin Laundry Association
1315 Butterfield Road, Suite 212
Downers Grove, Illinois 60515
Phone: (312) 963-5547
Members: Manufacturers–60, Distributors–200,
    Laundry Owners–2,800

American Coin-Op Magazine
500 North Dearborn Street
Chicago, Illinois 60610
Phone: (312) 337-7700
Circulation–18,085

Canadian Cleaner and Launderer
CTJ, Incorporated
One Pacifique
St. Anne de Bellevue, Quebec, Canada H9X 1C5
Phone: (514) 457-2347
Circulation–8,000

Coin Launderer & Cleaner
4512 Lindenwood Lane
Northbrook, Illinois 60062
Phone: (312) 272-8490
Circulation–22,914

Associations and Publications

National Coin-Operators Reporter
717 Chelten Avenue
Philadelphia, Pennsylvania 19144
Phone: (215) 843-9795
Circulation–18,000

New Era Laundry and Cleaning Lines
22031 Bushard
Huntington Beach, California 92646
Phone: (714) 962-1351
Circulation–26,130

Western Cleaner and Launderer
Wakefield Publishing Company
5422 North Figueroa Street, Suite 19
Los Angeles, California 90042
Phone: (213) 254-2320
Circulation–10,980

INDEX

Index

Index

Index

Index

Index

Notes

Notes

Notes

Notes

Notes

Notes

Notes

Notes

ORDER FORM

Please send _____ copies of **Coin Laundries: Road to Financial Independence** @ $29.95 including postage. Payment is to be made as follows:

[ ] My personal check is inclosed.

[ ] Please charge my: [ ] MasterCard   [ ] VISA

Card Number _ _ _ _ – _ _ _ _ – _ _ _ _ – _ _ _ _

Expiration Date _____

Signature _____

Name _____

Street Address _____

City & State _____ Zip Code _____

Telephone (___) _____

For faster service, credit card orders may be placed by telephone.
Call (503) 628-3995

MOUNTAIN PUBLISHING

P. O. BOX 1747-B   HILLSBORO, OR 97123

ORDER FORM

Please send _____ copies of **Coin Laundries: Road to Financial Independence** @ $29.95 including postage. Payment is to be made as follows:

[ ] My personal check is inclosed.
[ ] Please charge my: [ ] MasterCard   [ ] VISA
    Card Number _ _ _ _ - _ _ _ _ - _ _ _ _ - _ _ _ _
    Expiration Date _____
    Signature _____

Name _____
Street Address _____
City & State _____ Zip Code _____
Telephone (_____) _____

For faster service, credit card orders may be placed by telephone.
Call (503) 628-3995

MOUNTAIN PUBLISHING
P. O. BOX 1747-B   HILLSBORO, OR 97123

ORDER FORM

Please send _____ copies of **Coin Laundries: Road to Financial Independence** @ $29.95 including postage. Payment is to be made as follows:

    [ ] My personal check is inclosed.
    [ ] Please charge my: [ ] MasterCard   [ ] VISA
        Card Number _ _ _ _ – _ _ _ _ – _ _ _ _ – _ _ _ _
        Expiration Date _____
        Signature _____

Name _____
Street Address _____
City & State _____ Zip Code _____
Telephone (___) _____

For faster service, credit card orders may be placed by telephone.
Call (503) 628-3995

MOUNTAIN PUBLISHING
P. O. BOX 1747-B   HILLSBORO, OR 97123